The View From The Blanket

Weekapaug

Tom Zalaski

Michael and Tom Zalaski in Weekapaug

First Published in 2004

ISBN 978-1-539-4408-8-8

Printed in the United States of America

Acknowledgements

For a television newsman who has anchored well over 50,000 newscasts during the past 40 years, the idea of writing an acknowledgements page to *begin* this book is a foreign one. You see, in television news, we run the acknowledgements at the *end* of the show. We call them the *credits* which include the names of the show's producer, director, technical director, audio person, camera operators, videotape operator and floor director. The fact that our newscasts are live also affords us the luxury of pulling the plug on the credits if the show has not gone particularly well. More than once a producer has been known to scream, "Kill the credits! I don't want my name on this mess!" sparing the egos of those involved.

In the world of book writing there is no such safety valve. The credits or in this case, acknowledgements, are virtually etched in stone and there is no killing them. A book's acknowledgements also signify boldness, bravado and confidence on the part of the author who is essentially saying to the reader, "You're going to love what you're about to read and here is a list of the people who helped bring it to you." If the reader doesn't love it the acknowledgees have already been exposed and there is no ego-saving safety valve.

So it is with boldness, bravado and confidence that I say thank you to the following:

My friend and author Ellen Rosewall whose book, *Sparkle Island* provided me with motivation and ideas for mine.

Josh Zalaski, my brother, for his photography, advice and for listening to me read chapters ad nauseam over the telephone in search of his approval.

Joseph A. Zalaski, Jr., my father, who had the presence of mind on that August day in 1967 to grab the camera while everyone else on the beach could only stand dumbfounded during the shark invasion.

Arnie Banola for his knowledge of early family history in Weekapaug which was the foundation for the chapter entitled *How We Got Here*.

Aunt Kay Tronsky for her recollections included in the chapters *How We Got Here* and *The Cottage Is Gone!*

Chris DiPaola, Vito DiPaola, Lou Masucci and the gang at WBLQ-FM

Westerly, RI, for graciously plugging my book and for allowing me the privilege of guest-hosting the Saturday morning sports talk show.

The Bristol Press, Bristol, CT and Publisher William E. Sheedy for permission to reprint the article*'400 Pound Shark Reported By Terryville Girl'*.

Charlie Maggs of the New Weekapaug Bait & Tackle Shop for permission to reprint the tide chart.

WFRV-TV 5 (CBS), Green Bay, WI, Vice President/General Manager Perry Kidder and News Director Lee Hitter for use of the studio for my bio photo.

Peter and Wanda Barbeau and Jeff and Terri Koepper. The four of you *are*

Weekapaug and you were in my thoughts with each word I put to paper.

Anne and Bill Murphy, Maspeth, NY, for a Mountain of motivation. Listening to your music videos during the writing of this book allowed me to enjoy two of the great loves of my life simultaneously -- Weekapaug and Mountain.

Amy Crane Johnson, my editor at Raven Tree Press, Green Bay, WI, for not only helping me navigate shark-infested grammatical waters but also for her invaluable advice to a novice author.

Joe Rugowski and Monica Knutson, Digital Design Services, Inc., Green Bay, WI. Without your computer savvy and genius this book could not have been published. Thanks also for putting your special touch to all of the photographs herein. Joe, your magic on the dedication photo deeply moved me.

My friend and co-worker George Reed, former Creative Director, WFRV-TV, whose creativity and computer talents were always there for the asking. It is an honor for me to be able to say that a two-time Emmy Award winner had a hand in this work.

Leslie West, whose *Nantucket Sleighride* is part of my soul. When you introduced me to the *Mississippi Queen* in 1969 I had no idea I'd still be 'gettin' my kicks' with her more than 40 years later.

Anthony Robbins, whose *Personal Power* really works! This book proves it.

To Karen

Who once graced these beaches and who is now in the only place more beautiful than Weekapaug.

Thank you for Michael.

Table of Contents

Introduction

Everyone has their own Weekapaug. Where is yours? Think of the word Weekapaug as a metaphor for that special spot on earth which just the thought of results in pleasant, warm, happy, nostalgic memories that make you long to be there. Maybe your Weekapaug is Aunt Sarah and Uncle Bill's farm. Your summertime visits there as a child were a time to connect with cousins as you climbed up to the loft of the barn, fed the horses and played with the cats. Weekapaug is that dark, damp, musty cottage on a riverbank. Your grandparents bought the place back in the 30's and it has remained in the family ever since. On summer weekends and holidays it is the place where brothers, sisters, aunts, uncles, nieces and nephews gather for corn roasts, whiffleball and gliding down the river on inner tubes. At some point during the day Grandpa puts his bathing suit on, grabs a bar of Ivory soap and takes a bath in the river. Weekapaug is the deer hunting cabin your father brought you to on your first hunt when you were 12 years old. Now that you're an adult you realize it is not the hunt that brings you back here but rather the camp stories, the memories and most of all, to continue that special bond that began here so many years ago between you and your now aging father. Weekapaug is the week you spend at the cottage on the lake where your most important task is driving your boat over to your neighbor's dock to see if he wants to take a ride across the lake with you to have a cold one at the Fin 'n Feather.

We all have our own Weekapaug. It is not just a place we visit for a week or two each year. It is a place in our heart, our blood and our very soul that we can escape to 365 days a year simply by thinking about it.

My Weekapaug is a seaside hamlet on Rhode Island's coast. It is as small and quaint as its name sounds. Its pristine beaches and rocky shorelines are protected by ever-shifting, wind-laced sand dunes. Weekapaug is one of seven villages or fire districts that comprise the Town of Westerly, Rhode Island. A mile down the coastline from Weekapaug is another of the seven villages -- Misquamicut

-- whose state beach attracts thousands of people each day. Five miles further along the coast is the exclusive harbor resort community of Watch Hill. A short drive along Scenic Route One brings you to the quintessential New England fishing villages of Galilee, Point Judith and Narragansett. The historic whaling village of Mystic and its seaport is a 20-minute drive into Connecticut on I-95.

While Westerly's population is just over 22,000, I don't know the official population count of year 'round residents for whom this approximately two-square miles of oceanside turf known as Weekapaug is home. The U.S. Census Bureau puts the number at somewhere around 4,000 people. My unofficial estimate says that depending upon the season Weekapaug is either booming or boarded up. From mid-April to Labor Day Weekapaug experiences a population explosion. Rental cottages are booked solid, a sea of humanity covers the beaches and main roads into Weekapaug and Misquamicut are backed up for miles with carloads of people who don't necessarily have a cottage but who want to spend a day at the beach nonetheless. The outdoor decks of seaside restaurants are filled with people worshipping at the altar of a plate of steamers or lobster in drawn butter while watching the waves roll in. Convenience stores, souvenir stands, coffee shops and seaside restaurants are busy from sunup to sundown. The open ocean, bays and channels are filled with boats, kayaks and jet skis while on the shorelines you will find fishermen casting their sea poles while children scan the rocks and shallows for crabs and starfish. Much of Weekapaug is on a peninsula whose three sides are surrounded by the Atlantic Ocean, the Winnapaug Salt Pond and the Weekapaug Breachway.

I am glad my friends and coworkers have never been to Weekapaug and don't even know where it is. It's not that I wish to deny them the pleasure of spending two weeks here although as far as I'm concerned the fewer people who know about this place the better. It is just that they wouldn't understand what it is about this place that brings me back year after year. They would look for the Hyatt or the Sheraton and find neither. Upscale restaurants don't fit here either. Nor do trendy tourist shops. What draws me here is the rugged simplicity of this coastal New England village.

When my coworkers talk about *their* vacations I feel like an outsider who is out of touch with the way normal people spend their cherished vacation

time. Lisa spent two weeks doing missionary work with her parents in Africa. Erin went to Cancun. Jim experienced Italy this year. Other of my newsroom colleagues spent time in places like New York City, London, Chicago and Los Angeles. Imagine trying to explain Weekapaug to these world travelers! Any attempt at explanation would be futile. How do I make someone understand the grip that the deep, cold, mysterious, ominous and unforgiving great North Atlantic Ocean has on my soul? How do I describe the amazing experience of stumbling upon a prehistoric horseshoe crab? What words do I have to explain the feeling of dislodging a quahog from the sandy ocean floor? How do I describe the awesome power of a wave crashing against the breachway rocks at full high tide? Would my friends understand the thrill of watching a crab scurry across my path as I wade in knee-deep water or the early morning call of a seagull welcoming me to a new day? Would they be mesmerized as I am when I hear the distant warning cry of the foghorn as I look out on the fog-shroudded sea?

Weekapaug is not a place to be described. Weekapaug is a feeling. It is a feeling that lasts not just for a two-week vacation. Weekapaug is a feeling that can be tapped into in January in the middle of your worst day at work. The simple thought of Weekapaug, yours or mine and all it means to you somehow gives you momentary solace from the travails at the office.

For me, Weekapaug is the one constant in an otherwise chaotic year. It is an oasis where life's responsibilities and obligations cannot touch me. It is also a retreat where I am able to engage in deep thought about my life, the year ahead, my goals, my blessings and who I hope to be the next time I come here. I leave rejuvenated, armed with a new outlook on life. I am bursting with energy, confidence and invincibility as I charge toward the unfulfilled goals and dreams I so deeply contemplated. If only this feeling wouldn't diminish and die with the onset of winter's cold.

Weekapaug holds an extra special place in my heart because it serves not only as a vacation destination but also as the scene of our annual family reunion. My home in Green Bay, Wisconsin is 1,200 miles from Weekapaug. Most of the rest of my family lives in Connecticut. Each year during the first two weeks of August the Zalaski clan invades Weekapaug and inflates the population by at least 35 people. Although I do not see my five brothers and sisters, parents, nieces, nephews and cousins during the rest of year, our simultaneous arrival does not trigger wild emotional outbursts and shrieks and cries of, "Let me look at you!" As we greet each other for the first time in a year and exchange hugs a comfortable, knowing, secure feeling comes over us. We're all healthy. We all look great. We're here again. We're together. We're in Weekapaug.

Weekapaug is the place I last spent special times with some of my aging relatives who have since gone to their rest. It is also the place where several times in recent years I laid eyes for the first time upon a newborn niece or nephew.

I hope as you read these tales and essays about *my* Weekapaug that you find yourself being reminded of yours. I hope as you turn each page you find yourself saying, "That's exactly what we do!", "I've had that same feeling.", "His vacation sounds just like ours.", or "I thought only *our* family did that stupid stuff!"

I've never been to your Weekapaug nor you to mine. Yet, the map to both is the same. Follow your heart.

Everybody has their own Weekapaug. I welcome you to mine.

Nick and Kay Tronsky's cottage on Breach Drive

How We Got Here

World War II and a bowling ball led my family to this paradise we call Weekapaug.

In the early 1950's my great uncle Nick Tronsky was the five-time National Duckpin Bowling Congress Male Bowler of the Year. To this day there is an annual bowling tournament that bears his name -- The Nick Tronsky Unisex Doubles held each year in early February at the Holiday Lanes in New Britain, Connecticut. Uncle Nick is also listed on the CNN/Sports Illustrated internet website as one of Connecticut's 50 Greatest Athletes. He stands among the likes of Norwalk's Bruce Jenner who won the Olympic decathlon gold medal in 1976, San Francisco 49er quarterback Steve Young from Greenwich, New York Mets Manager Bobby Valentine from Stamford, skater Dorothy Hamill of Greenwich, former Boston Red Sox and New York Mets player Mo Vaughn who hails from Norwalk and golfer Julius Boros of Fairfield. Even after Uncle Nick relinquished his title he was still a regular fixture on television bowling shows. In the early 60's when I was nine or ten years old I sat in front of the television every Saturday morning to watch Uncle Nick bowl on one of those 'Bowling For Dollars' shows. Each week's winner won $1000 and the right to come back the following week to face a new challenger. The loser won a $500 consolation prize and the right to go home. During one incredible stretch Uncle Nick stood in victory lane nine consecutive weeks. I will never forget crying silently in front of the television on week 10 when Uncle Nick was defeated. However, $9,500 in 10 weeks wasn't bad money in 1960. That works out to an annual salary of more than $50,000 which, even today, some 40 years later, is a respectable wage.

In the late 1930's, this up-and-coming bowling phenom still had to have a 'real' job to support the family and put food on the table so he worked at Pratt and Whitney, a Windsor Locks, Connecticut-based manufacturer of aircraft parts. As World War II approached Nick was transferred to another Pratt and Whitney facility and he and his wife Kay took up residence in Westerly, Rhode Island. It was during this time that Nick and Kay discovered a nearby seaside hamlet called Weekapaug and they began frequenting its quaint beaches. In about 1950 when a cottage came up for sale, (Aunt Kay thinks a divorce played a role in its availability) Nick made a down payment of $500 with money he had won in a recent bowling tournament. Friends and relatives would visit the Tronskys at their seaside retreat and soon these friends and relatives began renting cottages in the area each summer. Things began to snowball. Kay's sister Anna and husband Joseph began renting as did three of Anna and Joseph's grown children -- Lillian, Joseph Jr., Henrietta and their families. I am one of Joseph, Jr.'s six children. My two sisters, three brothers and I represent the latest generation that continues the annual Weekapaug pilgrimage. The children of my sisters, brothers and I are all grown and now there are grandchildren. They will continue the tradition.

Uncle Nick died in 1989 at the age of 79. Aunt Kay was with us until 2006. Their Weekapaug legacy is also with us.

The improbable journey of Nick and Kay's cottage

The Cottage Is Gone!

Uncle Nick and Aunt Kay's cottage is located on what is essentially the tip of an oceanside peninsula. The cottages on Breach Drive are surrounded on three sides by the Winnapaug Salt Pond, the Weekapaug Breachway and the Atlantic Ocean. This peaceful, idyllic setting is a vacationer's dream, except for that day in 1955 when it became a watery nightmare. Hurricane Carol of 1954 ravaged the area. The cottages on Breach Drive, sitting exposed and completely unprotected on the peninsula were at the mercy of the high winds, storm tides and floodwaters.

At the time, the Tronsky's cottage boasted a fireplace which necessitated a large fireplace chimney. The luxury of a cottage fireplace is a rarity even today. However, it was that luxury that caused the cottage to take a most improbable journey.

As impossible as it may seem, the floodwaters got so high, water came down the fireplace chimney and filled the cottage. What happened next was even more amazing. The cottage was lifted off its foundation and floated across Breach Drive and then headed toward a row of cottages on the other side of the street. But the head-on, destructive collision with another cottage one would logically expect never happened.

Instead, the Tronsky's cottage somehow wiggled between two cottages and continued sailing into their backyards. The trip was not over. The cottage was then carried across the Weekapaug Breachway and was set down on Weekapaug Road on the other side of the breachway.

When the floodwaters had subsided and the cottage could be inspected for damage, Nick and Kay were relieved to discover that beside a few broken windows and some wet furniture the cottage was none the worse for wear. The task now was to return the cottage to its rightful address on Breach Drive. But how? Floating it back the way it came was obviously not an option. The only way back was to transport the cottage via the Weekapaug Bridge 200 yards away from where the cottage was set down on Weekapaug Road.

The Weekapaug Bridge is a narrow, two-lane span with a four-foot high cement railing on each side. How could a cottage that was obviously wider than the bridge be brought across without first cutting the building in half? The solution was to make sure that when the cottage was placed on the back of a flatbed truck, that the building was propped up higher than the bridge's four-foot high railings.

So for about $1000 the Tronsky's cottage made its journey home. From its Weekapaug Road post-flood resting place, the cottage was driven down the road, made a right turn onto the bridge and across the breachway, another right onto Breach Drive and was set back down on a new stone foundation.

Something even more horrific happened on that day in 1954 at a cottage just a few doors down from Nick and Kay's. I cannot verify this incident through public records or newspaper accounts. My sources of information are my now-deceased grandparents and aunts and uncles who remembered the day and whose memories I have no reason to question.

A cottage just down the street from Nick and Kay was rented by a family whose members included an invalid woman. On the morning of the flood, the family left the cottage by car to perhaps do some grocery shopping or to take care of some business back home in Connecticut. No one will ever know the actual reason for their excursion that day. As they left the cottage, they could not have known that the morning's showers would turn angry and become the Flood of '54. The invalid woman stayed at the cottage, lying on a small bed.

The water rose. It reached into the cottage and covered the floors of the kitchen, the living room and the bedrooms. The water continued to rise, lifting the bed with the woman on it off the floor. As the hours passed and the water rose the woman floated closer and closer to the ceiling. One can only imagine what was going through her mind. She no doubt assumed her family did not know the gravity of her situation. No one knew. No help was coming and a horrible death was inevitable.

However, the family did contact authorities and the Coast Guard raced to the cottage by boat and cut a hole in the roof. There they found the woman, still lying on the bed, nose pressed to the ceiling. I can only imagine the family's joyful reunion later that day.

The Weekapaug Bridge

The Weekapaug Bridge I

The Weekapaug Bridge that spans the Weekapaug Breachway is the physical and mental door which upon opening and going through, allows me to officially begin my vacation. As I drive from Dunn's Corners down Weekapaug Road the anticipation starts to build. By the time I reach the traffic light at the big old tree at Langworthy Farm I barely have the presence of mind to wait for it to change to green.

Just 30 seconds later I drive past Cove Road and instinctively look to the right. The Weekapaug Breachway. The water is like glass and a glance at the watermarks on the rocks on either side of the breachway tells me how close it is to either full high tide or complete low tide. As I look across the breachway I can see the cottages on Breach Drive and I know exactly what's going on in those cottages at this very minute. The renters are frantically cleaning and packing to beat the 11

A.M. zero hour at which time they must be out. They've had their two weeks. It's our turn.

My eyes now turn forward, down the breachway toward the ocean and there it is - the Weekapaug Bridge. It looks the same as it did last year and the 40 years before that. Light gray cement. See-through cement slats. Huge cement pilings sitting in the water to support the structure. It is as if the postcard picture I dream of each day of the year has suddenly come to life right before my eyes. This living postcard also speaks to me and says, “You’re here for another year. You made it. Welcome back.” My heart races as I turn right onto the two-lane bridge at which point I look at the faces of the drivers coming toward me in the opposite lane. They don’t look happy. They have the same cartop carrier on their roof as I do.

Their car is full of kids as is mine. Both of our back seats and trunks are filled with bags and boxes. But there is one big difference. They’re leaving and I’m just arriving! They are facing a night of seven loads of wash, vacuuming a sand-filled vehicle and packing away the cartop carrier, beach umbrella, rafts, goggles, nets and fishing poles for another year. They will sleep tonight in their Connecticut, New York and Massachusetts homes in places like South Windsor, East Hartford, Litchfield, Springfield, Plainville, Long Island, Tarrytown and Torrington. I’ll think of them at 11 o’clock tonight as I nurse a cocktail on the front porch of my cottage. Dinner this evening will be on the back patio of Paddy’s Wigwam overlooking the ocean or perhaps it will be on the deck of the Andrea Hotel or at the Pleasant View Inn. There is something special about that first night at the beach. There is something special about the bridge that got me there.

Inscription on the Weekapaug Bridge

The Weekapaug Bridge II

Although I have crossed the Weekapaug Bridge countless times by car and foot I can never remember the words that are engraved on the plaque that is embedded into the bridge. During my vacation in 2002 I made it a point to take particular notice of it. It says

WEEKAPAUG BRIDGE 1936
REPLACES STEEL BRIDGES ERECTED HERE IN 1898 AND 1918 AND A WOODEN TOLL BRIDGE ONE THIRD OF A MILE UPSTREAM

BUILT ABOUT 1880 FOR THE HAULING OF SEAWEED
BOARD OF HIGHWAY COMMISSIONERS FOR THE TOWN OF WESTERLY HARVEY C. PERRY, CHAIRMAN RALPH L. SEGAR, JOHN PUCCI, HOWARD W. CONGDON, ENGINEER

Although I said my trips across the bridge were countless, I have come up with a formula that gives me a pretty good guesstimate of the very minimum number of times I've crossed it. I am 50 years old at this writing and have vacationed in Weekapaug for two weeks and sometimes three each year for most of those 50 years. I know that in my younger years I made the trip two, three and even four times each day in order to get to Lamb's General Store for candy and comic books. But for the sake of a conservative average let's assume I walked across the bridge once each day everyday I have ever vacationed in Weekapaug. Fifty years at 14 days each year makes 700 trips. Since of course, crossing the bridge one way means you must eventually come back the other way, I have crossed the bridge at least 1,400 times. This number does not include the times I have driven a vehicle over the bridge in the 30-plus years I have held a driver's license. Adding in this number would easily put me over the 10,000 mark!

I am sure that depending upon one's age, their number of bridge crossings would be proportionately equal to mine. Yet, it amazes me how after hundreds, even thousands of crossings, walking across the Weekapaug Bridge is still an exhilarating, wondrous, breathtaking stroll even though nothing much about it has changed since the first time I walked across.

As you approach the sidewalk on the bridge you notice tiny shards of thick, broken glass on the span's asphalt pavement. I used to think this broken glass was the handywork of day visitors to Dunes Beach or Misquamicut State Beach who had had too much to drink and smashed their empty beer bottles on the bridge as they left. I was wrong and now humbly apologize to the patrons of Dunes Beach and Misquamicut State Beach. I am now quite convinced the glass got there for a totally innocent reason. I believe the glass came from some poor daytripper's automobile headlights or tail lights. Each day at about 3:30 the Weekapaug Bridge is backed up with traffic as the Dunes Beach and Misquamicut State Beach daytrippers make their way back to I-95. As they sit in their cars on the bridge waiting for their turn at the stop sign they strain for a last look at the water, the boats, the tide and people fishing. All it takes is one moment of inattentiveness to plow into the car in front of you and smash one, if not both of your headlights out or the tail lights of the car in front of you.

The Weekapaug Bridge isn't something you walk across just to get from point A to point B (i.e. to get across the breachway). There is an unwritten maritime rule that says you must stop halfway across, lean over the cement railing and stare into the water below. Just a few feet away from you is a young boy fishing from the bridge. The outgoing tide has pulled his line tight, giving the appearance that a trophy striped bass is on the other end. You cannot resist peering into the boy's plastic white bucket nearby containing what you assume to be the day's catch. You immediately realize this bucket contains no fish, just bait -- things like eels, frozen squid, leeches and minnows. You, being the compassionate sort, don't have the heart to tell the young man that the bait in his bucket and the lure at the end of his fishing pole are larger than any creature in the water below.

A pleasure boat approaches the bridge and just before it passes under, those aboard and those of us on the bridge exchange obligatory waves. We don't know each other. We're all just happy that for yet another year we made it to the Weekapaug Bridge.

Grocery Shopping

It doesn't matter who you are or how many years you've been coming to the beach, your vacation must begin with a necessary evil -- grocery shopping. What makes this chore particularly distasteful is that it must be done on your first day of vacation soon after you arrive. The last place you want to be on this precious day is in a grocery store. From the moment you left your home this morning to make your vacation drive your focus has been on beating the traffic, getting the cottage key, unpacking and mixing that first "we're here!" cocktail. However, the celebration must wait.

What makes the supermarket excursion even more painful is knowing that much of what you buy today will be thrown out in the trash in two weeks on the day you check out of the cottage. You essentially have to buy everything that you have in your refrigerator at your home. After all, you are going to be here for two weeks. Since dining out for three meals a day all 14 days is neither feasible nor fiscally prudent, you are faced with the fact that cooking will be a necessary part of this vacation.

Those of us who are vacation veterans arrive with a grocery list in hand -- one we made out at home. We know every item we will need, up to and including the salt and pepper. Such a list makes this excruciating excursion a bit more palatable.

The following are the items I will purchase on day one of my vacation that I know will be tossed out in the garbage on day 14: Hellmann's Mayonnaise, mustard, ketchup, cottage cheese, sour cream, yogurt, sliced or brick cheese, milk, coffee creamer, eggs, pickles, cold cuts, fruits and vegetables, ice cream, frozen pizza, salad dressing and two sticks of butter.

As I stand in the checkout line I think to myself, "This is not how I wanted to spend the first $200 of my vacation money."

Once the groceries are loaded into the car all seems right with the world once again. You've weathered the necessary evil of grocery shopping and your kids are in a frenzy because they think the next stop is the cottage!

Sorry kids. One more stop. Stay in the car. Mom and Dad will be out in 5 minutes. Ocean State Liquor. Vacation has officially begun!

The Laundromat

The necessary evil of grocery shopping on vacation has an 'evil twin' -the trip to the laundromat. Most cottages do not have a washer and dryer. If a cottage does have a washer and dryer they are usually locked in a basement or utility room. The padlock on the utility room door is a dead giveaway. Of all the cottages I have rented there was one that actually had a washer and dryer which the renter could use. Although the ability to do laundry anytime I wanted was a godsend, the cottage was so dark, dingy, damp and outdated I would gladly have traded the luxury of laundry facilities for a place where I didn't wake up feeling like I was in a leaking pup tent. Most years I am in a washerless, dryerless cottage which necessitates at least one, and usually two trips to the laundromat during my two-week stay.

My frustration begins the minute I decide that I *must* do laundry *tomorrow*. 'Tomorrow' usually means the first Friday of vacation. Since checking into the cottage the previous Saturday we've been going through towels, underwear, socks, bathing suits, jeans and t-shirts Saturday, Sunday, Monday, Tuesday, Wednesday and Thursday. The laundry *must* be done Friday not only because you're running out of clothes but also because you want to have it over and done with by the weekend. Nevermind that on vacation weekends should signify freedom no more than any other day. However, your mind has been programmed to think in terms of a five-day workweek followed by two days of freedom and relaxation, so vacation schedule be damned, the laundry *must* get done before the weekend!

Now that I've decided tomorrow is *the* day the frustration continues as I ask myself several maddening questions. I know where I went to do my laundry last year. Is the place still in business this year or will I pull into the parking lot only to find a beauty salon in its place? I want to telephone the place to find out but there are two obstacles in my way. First, I never paid any attention to the name of the laundromat. It was just the 'laundromat'. I knew where it was and how to get there and that's all that mattered. I didn't care what the name of place was. So there was no way I could look the place up in the phone book to call and see if they were still in business and what their hours were. The second obstacle is even if I knew the name of the place, the most recent Westerly telephone book in my cottage is from 1996. What are the chances my laundromat was in business back then?

Now my frustration turns to the financial aspect of the laundromat experience. I can't remember how much it costs to wash a load of laundry. I also can't remember how much the dryer costs and how much dryer time you get for the money.

So, in preparation for tomorrow's laundromat trip, while my family and friends lounge on the beach or nurse cocktails at the cottage, I reluctantly get in my SUV and drive to the laundromat. As I pull into the parking lot my heart skips a joyful beat because the place is still there! The sign on the door says "Open 7 A.M. -Last Load in at 6 P.M." I promise myself I will not be here at six tomorrow night.

As I pull out of the laundromat parking lot and head back to my cottage I try to figure out how many quarters I will need for tomorrow morning's excursion. I glance at the cupholder in the car that doubles as a toll change container for our trip out here and I guess there are about 10 quarters in it. I also know the coffee cup at the cottage I've been throwing spare change into probably has another 10 quarters, so I feel pretty confident I have enough quarters to get me through. I'll find out later just how wrong I am.

I am determined that come Friday morning I will be the laundromat's *first* customer and hopefully the first one out. Thursday night I inform all of my family members that if they have any clothing they want washed the garments are to be stuffed into plastic garbage bags before tomorrow morning.

The Friday morning alarm goes off at 6:30 and while the rest of the family sleeps, I crawl out of bed to perform one of vacation's most hated tasks. I stare into the bathroom mirror and amaze myself with how many different directions my hair can stick up and out. I don't care what I look like -- I'm going to the laundromat. I load the plastic garbage bags that are full of dirty clothes into the car and head out into the morning mist and fog. I allow myself the luxury of stopping at Bess Eaton Doughnuts for a coffee-to-go and the morning newspaper. Caffein and *The Courant* will go a long way in getting me through the next three hours.

As I pull into the laundromat parking lot I find a parking space near the front door which tells me that I am the first one there. I unload my garbage bags from the backseat, haul them through the front door and look for four empty washing machines that are together. As I shake each bag into the machines I notice a couple of whites have found their way into the colored clothes. I don't care. This is vacation.

Once I've loaded the machines, I go back out to my vehicle to bring in the box of Tide. I am so proud of myself for having brought my own detergent as opposed to having to pay $2.00 in the laundromat vending machine for two ounces of the same stuff. I am especially proud that I also remembered to bring Bounce sheets for the dryer.

It is at this point I realize I severely underestimated my quarter requirements. Each washing machine requires six quarters per load. I have four loads which will require 24 quarters, or four more than the 20 I brought in from the car and the coffee cup at the cottage. This means I must risk dealing with the Change Machine. The Change Machine accepts $1, $5 or $10 bills. Since I know I still need four quarters to get all the washing machines going and I estimate I'll need several more for the dryers, I push a $5-bill into the slot. Nothing happens. No change. My $5 bill is gone. I must now go find 'The Lady'. No one has ever been able to determine whether The Lady is the owner, the manager or a minimum wage employee. She can be found in one of two places. Sometimes she's 'in the back' folding sheets, starching shirts, or steam-pressing business suits. The other place you'll find her is on the main floor of the laundromat where she's feeding a commercial client's laundry into the eight machines marked "Do Not Use -- Manager Only". I approach her and begin to state my case only to be interrupted in mid-sentence with "I'll be there in a minute." She finally comes to help me and listens to my plight only until she hears the word "change" at which time she turns and heads for the change machine. She brings out 'the key' and as she opens the machine she asks me, "Did you put any money in?" Within seconds she spots my $5 bill which is ripped, shredded and wrapped around some gears. She pries the offending bill out and presses a lever that causes the machine to spit out 20 quarters. As she hands them to me her glare says, "How can you be so stupid that you can't operate a change machine?"

I finally start the four washers and sit on a plastic chair near the clothes- folding table where I can finally enjoy my coffee and newspaper. I know that the next 25 minutes belong to me, my coffee and my newspaper.

However, there will be interruptions. The laundromat workers are constantly loading and unloading washers and dryers with the clothing of people who can afford to 'leave' their laundry.

Other laundromat customers begin to drift in with their bags and baskets of clothing. There are always one or two middle-aged men in shorts and t-shirts. These guys are either divorced or just never made it and are living in an apartment with no laundry facilities. Then there's the woman who chainsmokes cigarettes, prances around in her spandex and who actually buys Tide in the vending machine. Some of these people know each other which tells me they probably meet like this every week. I am sure they are looking at me and wondering who the stranger is.

Once my four washing machines have stopped running I seek out one of those baskets on wheels to haul my wet clothes to the row of dryers. I am never lucky enough to find four empty dryers in a row so I have to make a mental note that I have dryers 3, 13, 16 and 25. A quarter buys 20 minutes of drying time but knowing that I have wet towels and jeans I immediately plug each machine with two quarters for 40 minutes of drying time. I now have to figure out how I am going to kill the next 40 minutes. I have already read the newspaper and there are two cold swallows of coffee left in the bottom of the styrofoam cup. I am reduced to sitting in my car and listening to the radio for the next 35 minutes. As I sit behind the wheel my only entertainment is watching the new arrivals trudging in with their loads of laundry. It is now their turn to face the change shortage, the change machine, The Lady and the key.

After 35 minutes of listening to the radio I make my way back into the laundromat to check on my four dryers. Each one has two or three minutes left which gives me time to grab another basket on wheels in which to load my clothes and bring them to the folding table. Once I have piled all of my clothes on the folding table and begin folding I notice some of the jeans and towels are not quite dry yet. I don't care! I fold them anyway. I want out of there! With all the clothes folded I carefully stack them on the back seat of the car. My final task is to make one last check inside the laundromat to make sure I didn't forget my box of Tide, the Bounce and my plastic garbage bags. Being a considerate customer I drink the last cold mouthful of coffee and discard the styrofoam cup into the trash basket. Lastly, I collect up my newspaper and take it with me. It doesn't matter that I've already read it front to back. The thought of a bunch of laundromat strangers reading *my* newspaper just doesn't wash.

Sandy's Fruit Market

Why is it that when we go on vacation we have to load up on fruit and other produce from Sandy's Fruit Market on Post Road?

We don't eat this stuff the rest of the year when we're home but for some reason we are compelled to buy loads of healthy fruits and vegetables on the first or second day of our vacation.

The Stop & Shop supermarket is right across the street from Sandy's. They have the same fruits. The same vegetables. The same everything. But for some reason we think the fruit from Sandy's is somehow superior and has some healthy magic attached to it.

Midway through the second week of vacation comes the evening when you can't push the pot of spaghetti sauce and the 12-pack of Budweiser all the way to the back of the refrigerator. Something's blocking your effort. You reach back there and feel a plastic bag full of something mushy. It's the six tomatoes you had every intention of using to make those healthy lettuce and tomato sandwiches. The bag is leaking and drips on the refrigerator shelf and onto the floor as you hoist the mess to the kitchen sink. It is at this point you remember the dozen peaches and plums you put in the vegetable bin.

Under the cheese slices, the hotdogs and deli meats, there they are, sitting in a half-inch of sticky dark liquid. The bottom of each peach and plum is soft, brown and oozing. The onion, green pepper and cucumber that are also sitting in this rotten brine will have to go.

Do I buy fruit and produce from Sandy's? Yes. Will I continue to do so? Yes. Will you? Yes. It's vacation.

Vincent Gentile and his three best grinder customers

Vincent and the Breachway Market

Everyone who rents a cottage in Weekapaug knows the Breachway Market. It is located next to the Weekapaug Bridge across the street from the Dunes Beach.

For those of us old enough to remember Lamb's General Store on the other side of the bridge and mourned its closing, Breachway Market has more than filled that place in our hearts for the past 25 years.

For the children of the 70's, 80's and 90's, Breachway Market is what Lamb's was to us, the children of the 50's and 60's.

Since my parents, brothers, sisters, relatives and I always rented cottages on Breach Drive, two to three trips daily to Breachway Market was not uncommon as the store was nearly in our backyard. This is what vacation was all about. We would talk about the Breachway Market at home all year long.

I was in my mid-twenties during that summer 25 years ago when we made the transition from the out-of-business Lamb's to Breachway Market. Each time I entered Breachway Market I could count on seeing the same lady behind the cash register. It was also a given that the same guy would be behind the meat counter year after year. He stood about 5'9", wore a white meatcutter's apron and always sported a baseball cap that said either "Weekapaug" or "Breachway Market". He had a very light complexion, almost pale which I found to be ironic seeing that his workplace was so connected to the sun and surf of Weekapaug. For some reason he reminded me of Uncle Charlie on the 60's TV show 'My Three Sons'.

Year after year without fail, the moment I set foot in Breachway Market on my first day of vacation Uncle Charlie would be there slicing meat and making grinders. 'Grinder' is the east coast term for submarine sandwich, hoagy or hero. The years were good to him. He never seemed to get any older. He always looked the same from year to year.

I would sometimes wonder why he stayed there for so many years. I assumed he was on an hourly wage so he probably wasn't getting rich at such a small market. I asked myself why he never moved on to bigger and better things. He was obviously a master at his craft and any large chain supermarket or packing house would have been wise to recruit a man of his talents. But then again, he was probably content working for the owner of Breachway Market, putting in his eight hours each day, leaving the headaches and responsibilities of the business to the absentee owner who probably visits the place once each year. Such was my thinking each time I entered the store between the early 70's and 1996.

In August of 1996 during my 44th summer in Weekapaug I walked into Breachway Market to order some grinders for my son and his friend. As the familiar meatcutter took my order and carried two large loaves of ham and turkey to the slicer I half shouted over the top of the meat case that separated us, "You make the best grinders in the whole United States!" I didn't know it, but at that moment a wonderful friendship was born. The man's head spun around and he flashed a huge smile. He dropped the two loaves of meat on the counter next to the slicer and walked toward me and over the top of the meatcase said, "Oh yeah? You like 'em?" I told him the number of years I had been coming to the store, that I was born and raised in Connecticut and that while my job brought me to Wisconsin I still came back two weeks each summer to Weekapaug and that his grinders were one of the highlights of our vacation.

He introduced himself as Vincent Gentile, who along with his wife Virginia, (the lady behind the cash register) *owned* Breachway Market! My jaw dropped as I realized that Uncle Charlie, the minimum wage meatcutter was a far cry from the chief cook and bottle washer for Fred MacMurray and My Three Sons -- he *owned* the house!

Each morning thereafter when I would go to Breachway Market for my *Hartford Courant* and *USA Today* the two of us would chat and in the process learn a little more about each other's lives. Then throughout the day members of my family would come into the store and introduce themselves with "I'm Tom's brother," "sister," "son," "nephew," "niece," "mother," "father," "godmother," "sister-in-law," "brother-in-law," or "cousin." After two days of this Vincent was convinced there were 100 of us!

Soon we all began to notice that when we ordered a large grinder, Vincent would pack it full, wrap it in white meat-wrapping paper, tape it and write the price of a *small* grinder on it. At least once each year a trip to the store for the newspaper found me walking out with five pounds of homemade soupy (Vincent's prize-winning sausage), or his homemade meatballs at no charge. The New York

The View From The Blanket strip steaks that were $7.99 a pound somehow showed up at the register at $2.99 a pound. One morning I bought four perfect New York strips for a barbeque later that evening. Vincent wrapped, taped and handed them to me. As I walked toward the cash register at the front of the store Vincent intercepted me and said he needed to talk to me near the door. When we got to the door I asked what he wanted. He said, "Have a nice day. Enjoy the steaks," and he pushed me and my money out the door toward my car.

Vincent even made the worst day of the year a joy. The worst day of the year is the Saturday that I must check out of my cottage, turn in the key, go back to my home and job and wait for 50 weeks until I can return. Each year, before my departure I stop in to the Breachway Market to say goodbye to Virginia and Vincent. Each year I walk out of Breachway Market with a large cardboard box loaded with huge grinders for me and three large teenage boys as we make our 1,200 mile drive back to Green Bay, Wisconsin. As you might have guessed, the bill is zero. We leave Weekapaug at about 11 in the morning and begin our 22-hour cross-country trek. You cannot imagine the joy 13 hours into the trip when it's midnight on the Indiana Turnpike and we break out Vincent's grinders!

Vincent and Virginia decided that the summer of 2002 would be their last at Breachway Market. Thankfully, the new owners have kept the place pretty much the same as when the Gentiles ran it. I continue to stay in touch with Virginia and Vincent through holiday greeting cards and telephone calls.

Vincent Gentile
December 6, 1922 - September 9, 2006
We miss you, Vincent

Cottage Drawers

There is something exciting and intriguing about opening all the drawers in the cottage before you fill them with your clothing and personal items. Regardless of how old you are, how many cottages you have rented or even if you rent the same cottage each year, this sense of wonder and anticipation is just as powerful every year. It is much the same as checking out the three or four drawers in a hotel room, only better. In the hotel room you pretty much know what you're going to find. In one drawer will be a Gideon's Bible. In another drawer you will find an impressive looking folder containing hotel stationery, envelopes and postcards. That's pretty much it. You stick the folder in your suitcase as a memento of your stay but otherwise you have no real attachment to anything you've found. Not so at the cottage! Every drawer is an adventure as well as a trip down memory lane because most of the same stuff that was in the drawers last year is in the drawers this year. You start with the bureaus and dressers in the bedrooms. The drawers are deep and wide and they make that empty, rumbling sound as you open and close them. You notice the bottoms of the drawers are lined with the same sticky paper as last year. And then there's the smell. Oh, that wonderful, musty smell! You can travel the world over but the only place you'll find that smell is in the cottage drawers.

You move to the kitchen and even though you know what is in every drawer you have to look in each one because by doing so you subconsciously assure yourself nothing has changed. Everything is the same as it was last year. This is the cottage as I've come to know and remember it. I am home. The utensil drawer has the same plastic divider -- knives, forks, teaspoons and tablespoons.

Somehow the serrated steak knives and the butter knives all wind up together. If you look closely you'll find there are parts of three different utensil sets that make up your vacation silverware. The drawer next to the silverware drawer contains the oversized spoons and forks for salads, pasta and the like. There is even a wooden spoon. There is usually a plastic spatula for baking as if someone is actually going to do any baking while on vacation. Then there is the eggbeater, the flat metal cheese shredder, a vegetable-peeling knife, a plastic ladle and a nutcracker. At home a nutcracker is for cracking nuts. At the beach a nutcracker is one of the most important ingredients in a lobster dinner. This drawer also contains two or three huge knives one of which is the size of a machete. I have no idea what these could possibly be used for. Now comes the drawer that contains the potholders under which are usually some hidden treasures like a book of matches, a corkscrew, two pennies, some garbage bag ties and the instruction booklets for the microwave oven and coffeemaker. This year, this particular drawer in my cottage contained the following items: coffee filters, a clothespin, two pink birthday candles, a black magic marker, a small bulb, instructions for the refrigerator, a vacuum bag, a paint stirring stick, a Phillips Tip screwdriver, two pens (one from Mohegan Sun Casino), Post-It-Notes, labels, a garbage tie, a bobby pin, thread, one penny, a nail and a AAA battery.

In each cottage there is usually a desk or a small hutch atop which sits the telephone. The drawer in this desk is the one that's most fun to open. This drawer contains the deck of playing cards from Ocean State Liquor, the latest copy of the Westerly Chamber of Commerce magazine, a Westerly telephone book that is at least six years old, a used miniature golf scorecard (Jeremy beat Ma, Paul, Dad and Erin), a map of South County, a brochure from the Mystic Aquarium, a menu from Papa Gino's Pizza and a metal thimble from someone's now-incomplete Monopoly game. Here is what I found in the drawer in the summer of 2000: The Westerly Area Phone Book (June 1996-May 1997), the Go Westerly Magazine (which comes in your rental folder packet), instructions in English and Spanish for the Sears vacuum cleaner, a menu from the New China Pavilion Restaurant, a notice that a census taker had been at the cottage, an Amtrak train schedule for Spring/Summer 1995, a 1995 Rhode Island Visitor's Guide, a clothespin, three placemats, two pens and an audio book cassette tape of 'Independence Day'. I think this year I'll leave something in the drawer like a lobster keychain or a champagne bottle cork. It'll make it more interesting for the next guy!

***A scene of ultimate peace and serenity from the* back porch of our cottage on the salt pond**

Why I Hate Golf

8-3-2000

I don't like golf, golfers and the whole golf culture. I find it no coincidence that country clubs look like and operate like plantations or that professional golfdom's premier event on the hallowed grounds of Augusta, Georgia is called ironically, The *Masters* Tournament. First, I don't view golf as a sport but rather an activity to be lumped in the same category as auto racing, bicycle riding and hunting. To qualify as a sport an activity must be one where someone is physically trying to prevent another person from reaching or accomplishing a goal. In baseball a pitcher will purposely throw close to a batter's head to intimidate him and make him a bit nervous about each subsequent pitch. A baseball catcher will collide head-on with a player who dares try to cross home plate from third base. Hockey players proudly display missing teeth. They have railroad track-like scars all over their bodies -- the result of countless stitches. Ask any professional basketball player about the perils of driving to the basket against 7'1", 315-lb Shaquille O'Neal.

A true sport is played amidst a fan feeding frenzy as they scream for blood, sometimes literally. A baseball batter knows all too well that a pitcher like Roger Clemens can, with surgical precision, take off the tip of your nose with his 95 mile-per-hour fastball. Imagine trying to concentrate as this white bullet called a baseball comes toward your head as 40,000 fans scream at the top of their lungs.

A wide receiver for the National Football League's New England Patriots runs a route over the middle of the field. As 60,000 fans scream, he leaps into the air, catches the ball and is immediately sandwiched in midair by two 250-lb defensive backs whose job it is to make sure the receiver can only exit the field by means of a stretcher.

Then there is the golfer. He sets the ball gingerly on a tee. The ball sits there until the golfer is ready to pummel it with a titanium club. This ultra high tech titanium club compensates for the golfer's total lack of physical strength. Teeing up the ball reminds me of when my son was seven years old and played tee-ball where a plastic whiffle ball is placed on a waist-high plastic tee so that the child can hit it from this stationary position as opposed to having someone pitch it to him. Golf is tee-ball for adults. Yet, in this game of adult tee-ball, silence is demanded and insisted upon! The click of a camera is the catalyst for a combination tirade and tantrum directed at the entire gallery from a professional golfer.

I could be persuaded to look upon golf more kindly if the plantations allowed cheering and heckling from the gallery as a golfer attempted to hit the ball. Until then, I can only take pleasure in watching these overweight, pasty white 'athletes' run around their "Minorities Need Not Apply" country clubs screaming "The sky is falling!" because a young African American by the name of Tiger Woods now dominates their game. You can just imagine one of these guys coming home from a day at the plantation playground and trying to explain the Tiger Woods phenomenon to his children. "Muffy, Tiffany, I don't quite know how to break this to you, but, oh my Gawd, the *busboy* has won the Masters."

What triggered this anti-golf outburst by yours truly? What does this have to do with Weekapaug, you ask? I just looked out the backdoor of my cottage and saw something that made me livid. I could have reacted in one of two ways.

My first instinct was to scream four-letter words and inflict bodily harm upon the culprit. My second choice was to grab a pen and pad and write about it. I know what they say about the pen being mightier than the sword but at that particular moment, if the truth be known, I'd rather have used the sword and written about it later.

As I looked out the backdoor of my cottage I laid eyes on the ultimate scene of peace and tranquility. This is the view I dream about during the 50 weeks of the year when I am not here. My cottage lawn leads to a stone wall with cement steps leading into the shallow salt pond. The pond is like glass. A crane flies low over the water. Two small islands just 30 feet offshore are teeming with seagulls pecking at mussels, clams and crab carcasses. Other seagulls are peacefully floating in the water patiently waiting for a school of unsuspecting minnows to swim past. One hundred yards beyond the islands are three black seabirds sunning themselves on what appears to be a huge log sticking out of the water. Just beyond the birds are people clamming in waist-deep water. With their clam rakes they carefully scrape the bottom of the pond in their quest of the hardshell delicacy.

In essence, the view before me is a living, breathing, moving postcard.

The View From The Blanket

Suddenly, this perfect moment turned chaotic as if God had grabbed it and shook it violently. The seagulls on both islands exploded skyward in unison. The seagulls that were floating on the pond saw the mass exodus and joined it a split second later. The black seabirds watched for a second, then, sensing danger they too took flight.

Empty islands. Barren water. A lonely log protruding from the water. No cranes flying low. Silence save for one sound. Whack! Whack! Whack! The sound pierced the air like a gunshot. I looked to my right into the neighbor's backyard where the sound was coming from and I was instantly overcome with rage. A Preppie Golfer Nerd had decided that the salt pond was his own personal driving range. Some of the balls he hit went 200 yards out into the pond. Some just 50 yards, landing in the knee-deep shallows. He topped two of them that dribbled off the tee, rolled to the stone wall and plopped into the water. One of his drives bounced off a boat-mooring pillar 20 feet offshore and ricocheted back nearly hitting him, the cottage and anyone who was nearby. My anger was further feuled by the fact that the property Preppie Golfer Nerd's cottage sits on borders the Winnapaug Country Club. One of the country club's greens is so close to the cottage that one could throw a golfball from the cottage's back porch into the hole. Yet, there he was, driving balls into the salt pond -- Mother Nature and the environment be damned.

Preppie Golfer Nerd was the typical junior exec with his Izod shorts and shirt, brand new tennis shoes and white socks. This is the guy whose only way up the corporate ladder is to golf with the boss every Thursday, making sure the boss always wins. Although he said nothing, each Whack! spoke volumes to me. Loudly and clearly I could hear him say, "I don't care about you, your vacation, nature, the environment, clammers, the law or other people's property."

It is illegal to hit golfballs into the salt pond. Golf balls have an acid core. A large fish such as a striped bass that mistakes the ball for food dies a slow, agonizing death. Clammers and bathers don't like stepping on golf balls. Owners of expensive boats parked on the pond do not relish the idea of dents or other damage to their crafts. The seagulls, seabirds and cranes shouldn't have to suddenly find themselves in the line of fire.

I was within a split second of treating him to a profanity-laced explosion. But just then he teed up another ball and I knew I had to be quiet.

Rainy Days

(Written 8-1-00, Day 10 of 12 days of rain)

There is nothing as miserable as a rainy day at the cottage. I can deal with fog in the morning because a morning fog burns off by ten or eleven o'clock and a great beach day awaits. Not so with rain. Beach rain that blows in off the ocean is unforgiving. There is no middle ground. No sprinkle. No light mist. A beach rain is a hard-driving, all-day affair and anyone who believes it's going to clear up by afternoon also believes his cottage rental rate will go down next year.

The minute you wake up and look out the window the beach rain starts talking to you. "You are going to have a miserable day," it says, "and nothing you do will change that fact so just get through it and get over it."

But you are not so easily discouraged. You look out the window again and tell yourself it will clear up by noon. Deep down, however, you're really not convinced so you look out of every window in the cottage -- east, west, north and south in search of any sign of clearing. But the view and the prognosis is the same at each window -- nothing but an unending gray sky. As if to rub salt in the wound the steady rain begins to fall harder. A steady stream of water cascades off the cottage roof and down over each door and window. To exit the cottage at this moment would be like walking under a waterfall.

Your next move is to grab the television remote control and turn on the Weather Channel where you see a map of Connecticut, Rhode Island, New York and Massachusetts covered in dark green signifying rain and clouds for the next 12 hours. Your response is, "What do those Weather Channel guys know? They're down in Atlanta, Georgia."

Your last resort is the local radio station and there is a spark of hope as the announcer intones, "High tide will be at 6:43, low tide at 12:51." You optimistically surmise that the reason the announcer is giving the times of the tides is because beach-goers will want to know. Thus, the announcer must have some reason to believe people will be on the beach later in the day. Your optimism is crushed as the announcer delivers his next line -- "100 percent chance of rain and thunderstorms today and tonight, tapering off to 80 percent tomorrow. Your four- day outlook doesn't get much better."

You finally resign yourself to the fact that this will be a day without sun, sand or surf and if this precious vacation day has any prayer of being resurrected it will be on your enterprising shoulders. The pressure on you to think of something increases exponentially with the number of young children in your cottage. It is at this point that panic sets in. You have been through this drill in past years and you know you are in a no-win situation.

You brought the VCR down for just such an occasion. But the kids have been watching tapes each of the four nights you've been here so rainy day or not, the VCR is no longer a novelty. Regular TV isn't the answer either. Unless the cottage has cable television, reception in most cottages is like watching a snowstorm, or, as we used to call it, 'ant fights.' If you suggest to the kids that they read a book I suggest you read an earlier line in this chapter about next year's rent going down. Not going to happen!

You quickly dismiss the breakfast in Watch Hill idea. Last year's rainy day wait at the Olympia Tea Room reminds you that everyone has the same idea as you. The idea of shopping in Watch Hill has two drawbacks. First, it is raining as hard in Watch Hill as it is at your cottage. Second, after you've pointed through the rainy car windshield at one of Watch Hill's claims to fame -- the United States' oldest (closed, rain-drenched) merry-go-round, your very unimpressed kids are ready to return to the cottage and clean their rooms just for a little excitement.

The Mystic Aquarium? You even laugh at yourself for that brainstorm. It would be wise to pack a picnic basket for the three hours you'll be sitting in traffic on I-95 waiting to reach Exit 90 for Mystic along with the 10,000 other people with the same rainy day idea.

Galilee? Rain. Narragansett? Rain. Charlestown? Rain. You never thought you'd say this but right about now you would welcome the threatened visit from your wife's brother and his family.

There is nothing as miserable as a rainy day at the cottage.

The cottages on Atlantic Avenue feature architecture ranging from quintessential New England to modern new millennium

A Drive Down Atlantic Avenue

You might call Atlantic Avenue the Gold Coast of Westerly, Weekapaug and Misquamicut. Atlantic Avenue begins at the Weekapaug Bridge and ends two miles later somewhere beyond the Andrea Hotel. Like most vacationers, I have never had a reason to continue past the Andrea so whatever lies beyond the grand hotel will forever remain a mystery to me.

Equally mysterious are the 'cottages' that line Atlantic Avenue. To call these places 'cottages' is like referring to Watch Hill as a quaint fishing village.

We all have driven this stretch of coastal road hundreds of times and whether you are on vacation at your cottage or 500 miles away sitting in your office at work daydreaming about vacation, you know every inch of Atlantic Avenue. We've all wondered about the Big Cottage -- that huge brown mansion that sits high atop a stone and rock wall. We ask ourselves, "Who lives there?" "Who owns it?" "What do they do for a living?"

As we drive on we marvel at the unique architecture of each place. Some are Old New England while others are ultra modern with odd-shaped windows, solar panels and winding staircases around the outside. Some have decks on the roof much like a crow's nest. Some roofs have what looks like a small lighthouse at the very peak. Each cottage is oceanfront, just yards away from the pounding surf.

We even envy the driveway entrances to these places. On each side of the driveway entrance will be either huge boat anchors or five-foot tall lighthouses. The fence posts are not connected by wooden boards but by nautical rope giving the front of the place the look of a ship's deck. We tell ourselves we're definitely going to do that at our home as soon as we return from vacation.

During the whole trip the kids are saying, "Mom, look at that cottage. Oh cool!" "Oh neat, look at that deck where they can sit and look out over the ocean!" "Oh God, look at the size of that place!" "Man, why can't *we* have a place like that?!" "How come we can't be rich like those people?"

Meanwhile, you drive on, thinking about your family, your vacation, your cottage, your job and your friends and how much these two weeks mean to you at which point you have the desire to tell the kids, "We're richer than those people will ever be."

But it's still okay to dream.

The five words dog owners do not understand

Dogs On The Beach

The silent majority has held its collective, polite tongue for too long and has now been pushed to the point of unleashing a not-so-subtle scolding to those of you who insist on bringing your dogs on vacation with you. We would like to teach you a word you have obviously never learned. Kennel. K-E-N-N-E-L. A kennel is a place that will board your dog while you are away. Kennel personnel will take care of your dog, feed it, give it water, exercise it, pet it, walk it and even talk to it in 'doggy talk' the whole time you are gone. If the word 'kennel' is too difficult for you to find in the dictionary perhaps you might try looking up 'neighbor' or 'relative'. These two entities can provide the same services as a kennel.

The best argument I can make for putting your dog in a kennel is that the rest of us vacationers won't have to suffer the inconsiderate and annoying presence of your dog on our vacation. When I see you walking your dog down the street I get the urge to follow you to see what cottage you're in. I certainly don't want that place next year. I wonder what the next occupants of your cottage would say if they saw your dog on the beds, the couch or even stretched out on the floor. No amount of cottage cleaning will rid the place of all the dog hair. God forbid if the next family to occupy the cottage has a child who is severely allergic to pet hair. But then again, you don't care.

You might make the argument that your 'Bonehead' is tied up outside and never comes into the cottage. How nice for the next renters as their children unsuspectingly walk barefoot on the lawn where Bonehead has done his business for two weeks.

You also have the audacity to bring your dog onto the beach to frolic in the water. First, it's illegal. Second, you have no idea how dangerous this is not just to the other people on the beach, but to you and your dog as well. I know that your Bonehead is friendly, has never bitten anyone and loves children. But remember, that's how your Bonehead acts when he is home, in a familiar house, in familiar surroundings with familiar people. Beachblanket Bonehead is a much different animal. There are hundreds of strangers around him, the surf is pounding, the wind is blowing and kicking up sand, children are waving shovels and pails, boogeyboarders are racing down the beach, a group of teenagers is playing football, and seagulls are divebombing the beach in search of popcorn, Cheeze-Its and pieces of grinder. Your calm, loving, gentle Bonehead is now a spastic bundle of nerves. He has never been in this situation before and you have no idea how he will react to the sudden movement of a stranger.

Now comes the real danger. Every parent on the beach who was reading a book, listening to the radio, playing cards or just taking in the sun is now on the edge of their seat as they see Bonehead get closer and closer to their children playing in the water or on the sand. Every mother turns to every father and says, "Honey, quick, go down near Emily. That big dog is coming and I'm nervous."

As a father who many years ago kept an eye on a young child on the beach I can tell you that in these situations fathers don't get nervous -- they get mad. We immediately plan our course of action should Bonehead lunge at our child or scare our child in any way. We fathers are generally a peaceful, gentle, loving, educated and law-abiding lot. Until Bonehead lunges at our kid. As we plan our course of action here are the questions we ask ourselves as we get ready to spring out of our beach chairs: "Am I going to drown the dog or grab it and break its neck? Will I kick him under his chin or will I drive my foot between his eyes to insure instant death? Will I strangle him with his own chain? And after I've done all that, will I step on his head and crush his skull in front of his owner?"

Then I'll go back to my blanket and continue with my crossword puzzle in the *New York Times*. Let's see, eight across, 'boarding facility', six letters, beginning with K and ending in L.

A tidepool

Tide Pool

It happens just once during your entire two-week vacation. Perhaps twice if you're lucky. It's a Thursday afternoon. You just took a quick dip in the surf and are now stretched out, face down on your blanket or towel. The beach is crowded with people, umbrellas, pails, shovels, blankets, beachbags, beach chairs and toys. You can hear the woman on the blanket next to yours yelling to her son, "Jimmy, you want a peach?" As Jimmy runs toward the blanket he kicks sand on your back and you hear him whine, "Don't we have any more Cheez-Its?"

This is your cue to take a walk on the beach. You're hot. You don't want to go in the water right now. You just need to cool off. You need to stretch, breathe and enjoy the sun. Ten minutes into your walk you suddenly realize you have left the crowds behind. No one is behind you and the only person coming in your direction is an elderly man wearing a golf cap who is intently scouring the beach for rocks and shells which he places in his plastic bag. You are the temporary owner, landlord, king or queen of this desolate stretch of beach.

You decide it might be fun to leave the firm, hard-packed sand which is still glistening from the last wave and continue your walk in crystal clear ankle-deep saltwater. After a few steps you decide to venture out further and you are soon moving at a much slower pace as you slosh through knee-deep water.

Suddenly, as if by magic, it appears before you -- a tide pool. It is as if somebody placed a 100' by 100' cereal bowl in the ocean and lined it with sand. Somehow, the white foam of the breaking waves knows not to disturb this pool and rushes past on either side. You walk to the very center of the pool and in doing so, walk back to your childhood.

You can feel the sun on your back and face as it creates a glare on the water. Through the water you can see your feet and toes more clearly than if you were sitting on the beach looking at them. The bottom of the tide pool is perfect. No rocks, stones, pebbles, shells or seaweed. The sand is rippled much like a desert landscape. Your only companions are the four minnows that dart past your knees, always moving a safe distance away each time you edge toward them.

The child in you tells you to sit or at least kneel in the water to get the full effect of the experience. For a few brief moments this tide pool is yours. No one is allowed into your perfect cereal bowl circle. A beachcomber or even a child had best not violate this space or this moment. It belongs to you and no one else.

As you rise to leave you have mixed emotions. You will cherish this experience each time you think about it in the coming year. You are also somewhat sad knowing that if you come back to this very spot tomorrow the tides will have reshaped the contour of the ocean floor and the tide pool will not be here.

Yet, you take heart because you know that next year at some point during your vacation you and the tide pool will somehow find each other.

Burlingame

I have never understood people who go to Burlingame. The Burlingame Campground at Burlingame State Park is a beautiful, oasis-in-the-woods campground on Route One about eight miles outside of Westerly and Weekapaug in Charlestown. I have friends who vacation there and they think it's wonderful. They eat, sleep and breathe Burlingame just as I eat, sleep and breathe Weekapaug all year long.

But why would you camp near an ocean? Why don't you go to Montana? Colorado? South Dakota? Maine? where you can hike and do outdoorsy, woodsy stuff?

Do you go to Mormon-influenced Salt Lake City to drink and gamble? Do you go to frozen, snow-covered Vail to soak in the sun and get a tan? Do you go to Bourbon Street for a religious revival?

Burlingame campers pump their water and then boil it. My cottage has faucets. Burlingame campers use outhouses. My cottage has indoor plumbing. Burlingame campers splash and play in the swimming hole at the center of the campground. I splash and play in the Atlantic Ocean at the center of the world. Burlingame campers shop at the camp store at the center of the campground. I shop at Benny's and Wal-Mart. Burlingame campers cook their food over campfires or on a grill. I eat at the Watch Hill Inn. Burlingame campers make s'mores and sing Kumbaya around the campfire at night. I make martinis and watch the Red Sox or Yankees on my cottage cable TV.

Visiting someone at Burlingame means suffering through a background check at the hands of Ranger Rick, the guardhouse rent-a-cop who pokes his head into your car window in search of contraband marshmellows. As I drive past the campsites, it seems everyone has a sign with their last name on it that they made during the winter with a woodburning set and shellac. The Johnson's. The Smith's. Invariably, the apostrophe is in the wrong place.

I must admit I do go to Burlingame once each year. It's the only place within 50 miles where you can purchase a two-week shellfish license to dig for clams.

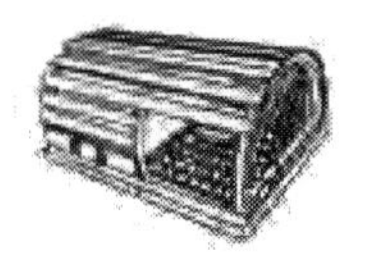

The Valet

I used to enjoy jumping in the car on any given afternoon and heading up Atlantic Avenue toward Misquamicut State Beach and the amusement park in search of a seaside restaurant where I could have a cold beer and a plate of steamers as I sat on the restaurant's back deck watching the waves roll in.

We'd park in the lot right next to the restaurant. Oftentimes, the parking space found my car positioned on a dune facing the ocean. When the car doors opened our bare feet would hit the combination sand and rocks, and we'd "oooh" and "ooww" our way into the place, sandy feet and all.

Inside would be people sitting at the bar in their wet bathing suits. The jukebox was filled with songs that brought you back to vacations of your childhood. All the windows were opened and from the inside you could see all the people sitting out on the deck. You could hear the waves. The atmosphere was so relaxed and informal. This is what I dreamed about all year long.

Then came that fateful afternoon when I pulled my car into the driveway of a restaurant two doors down from the amusement park. I had been here countless times. The establishment held a special place in my heart because this is where my father and I came one afternoon to savor cold beers and a plate of mussels. We gave our camera to the waitress and asked her if she would take our picture which she gladly did. To this day that picture is one of my most cherished -- Dad, me, beer, mussels, tans, the beach and a beach bar.

But on this day when I pulled my car into the driveway I was stopped by a young man who looked like a waiter in a high-class restaurant. He sported a white shirt, a bow tie, black pants and shiny shoes. He looked much like the groom at a wedding who had discarded the jacket of his tuxedo. He was there to park my car. He offered me some sort of ticket stub and told me he would bring my car around when I left.

I left. Right then. Three minutes later I was enjoying a Budweiser on the back deck at Paddy's where they still understood what the beach is all about.

Venting About Renting

Hurry Up And Wait

Over my many years in Weekapaug I have rented 10 different cottages. I have also spent a substantial amount of time in at least 10 others that were rented by my parents, sisters, brothers, relatives and friends. I find it interesting that each year regardless of what cottage we're in we all have the same observations, comments and complaints about our particular cottage. I would guess that your family and friends who rent are very much like mine. Thus, you probably have the same observations, comments and complaints and go through the same rituals that I do. Let's compare notes!

I always arrive early for my first day of vacation. Even though I know *exactly* how long the 1,200-mile drive takes to get from my home to Weekapaug, and even though I know that no matter what time I get there I *can't* get my cottage key from the realty office until 1 P.M., I reach the Westerly exit off I-95 at about 9 o'clock on Saturday morning. Thus, I have four hours to kill. However, after years of arriving early I have perfected the art of killing those four hours and I have it down to a science, almost to the minute.

When I first arrive in Weekapaug I can't resist slowly driving past my cottage and sneaking a peak. Are the current renters still there frantically trying to beat the 11 A.M. checkout deadline? Most times, however, it is the cottage owner's car I will spot in the driveway. How do I know it's the owner? The car is empty. There is no luggage rack or cartop carrier. There are no shirts or dresses hanging up clothesline-style across the back seat. The front door of the cottage is wide open and there is a cleaning bucket sitting on the porch. A broom leans up against the porch railing. Through the kitchen window of the cottage that I know so well I see someone standing over the kitchen sink. The owner is cleaning. But why? I thought the previous renters were supposed to clean the cottage before they checked out? If the previous renters cleaned the cottage even half as thoroughly as I will when I check out, the owner will have to do nothing more than a quick walkthrough for her own peace of mind.

I slowly drive past the cottage then head to downtown Westerly for breakfast at the Prime Time Cafe. It was only recently that I learned the Prime Time Cafe was not in Rhode Island at all and was actually located in Connecticut having fallen short of the Rhode Island border by about 20 feet. Thus, we park the car in Rhode Island and have coffee in Connecticut. We arrive at the restaurant at about 9:30 and by the time we've eaten and relaxed with coffee and conversation about our plans for the next two weeks, the clock reads 10:30 or 11:00. The next stop is the Stop & Shop supermarket on Post Road. By the time we have filled two grocery carts and received $1.33 in change from two $100 bills it is time to drive to the realty office to pick up the key. To an outsider the key is simply a cheap piece of metal attached to a piece of plastic with the cottage number on it. However, in your hand, the key turns to gold.

When I finally get into my cottage I immediately notice two things. First, the place looks pretty much the same as it did last year. All the furniture is in the same place, the same pictures adorn the walls, utensils, pots, pans and plates are all in the same drawers and cabinets and the closets are virtually void of hangers save two or three. The second thing I notice are the Cottage Rules posted either on the refrigerator or on a kitchen wall. This is the same list of rules I've been reading year after year and while I know it almost by heart I always read it again if only to find out when trash day is. Somewhere at the bottom of this typewritten page, written in the owner's handwriting is the 11th Commandment in capital letters -- PLEASE DO NOT PARK ON THE GRASS. This presents a major problem. The owner advertised the cottage as one that "Sleeps 8." Let's imagine that this cottage which supposedly sleeps eight is being rented by four couples who each come with their own vehicle. The driveway can accomodate two vehicles. But four cars need four parking spaces. Signs that line the street specifically state "No Parking -- Tow Away Zone." As I see it there are several solutions to this dilemma, some workable and some perhaps not. First, the eight people could rent a school bus and arrive en masse looking much like they were going to a Grateful Dead concert. Second, if the driveway cannot accommodate the number of vehicles eight people require, chauffeur or taxi service should be included in the rental price. On a more practical note how about a street parking system under which renters are issued a sticker to be placed on the inside of the windshield. The sticker, which would include the cottage name and address would let police know that the car is owned by a cottage renter. Why would town officials be opposed to legitimate renters parking on the street overnight? It's not as if the snowplows have to get through!

Trash

The Cottage Rules have specific instructions about trash disposal and how recyclables are to be separated. Trash pickup day is Tuesday. Tuesday?! Today is Saturday. The former renters who vacated the premises just hours ago have filled all the trash cans with spoiled food, rotting fruit, moldy cheese, cold cuts that have turned green and even disposable diapers. Cans and bottles are falling out of the overflowing recyclable bin and are all over the lawn. I have to live with this heap of someone else's trash for the next four days? Where shall I put my own trash? I can also be assured that by tomorrow morning the raccoons and skunks will have torn open every bag which means I'll be spending my first Sunday morning of vacation picking up chicken bones and Cheetos off the lawn. Considering what I'm paying for this place *daily* trash pickup shouldn't be a problem.

Sleeps *How* Many?

Some years I have found myself the victim of what I call the Cottage Capacity Con Job. The description in the rental agreement says my cottage "Sleeps 8." Eight what? Realistically, the place could sleep eight five-year olds. Their parents, however, would have to find a room at the Andrea Hotel or the Weekapaug Inn. One place in particular I rented had three bedrooms, each with an *alleged* double bed and also a pullout couch in the living room. The owners figured two people in each bed and two people on the pullout justified advertising the sleeping arrangements as accommodating eight people. The truth of the matter is that each bed could handle one adult and that's even a stretch if that one adult happens to be taller than six feet and weighs more than 200 pounds. The pullout is not large enough to accommodate even one body. For the person who winds up on the pullout couch, stretching out is out of the question. To stretch out fully would mean one's feet would hang off the end and nearly touch the floor. The person who gets stuck with the pullout is condemned to a night in the fetal position. And, just because there are two pillows on a bed doesn't necessarily mean the bed was meant for two bodies. The Cottage Capacity Con Job could be remedied if the owner would just once invite seven friends to spend the weekend.

Cleaning

Why is it my responsibility to clean the cottage when I leave? This is adding insult to injury. Checkout day in and of itself is the most miserable day of my entire year. I will not be back for 351 days. Before I set foot in the cottage again I will go to work 250 times, get the kids through another school year, weather another miserably cold and snowy winter and I will be a year older. It is somewhat like being condemned to Hell but being forced to clean Paradise before you leave so that others can enjoy it. I think the cottage owner should hire a cleaning service to do the dirty work. One recent year my cottage rental rate was $1,700 per week or $3,400 for two weeks. This works out to just over $240 per day. If I stayed at a motel or hotel for two weeks my rate would be only half that and not only would my room be cleaned each day, they'd leave two mints on my pillow along with a note saying "Thank You For Staying With Us."

Prior to the beginning of the summer rental season every cottage owner should be required to collect all the cleaning items and products that are in the cottage and try cleaning their own homes with them. Cottages come equipped with one of two types of vacuum cleaners. One is the 50-pound monstrosity that's about 20 years old and requires two people to push it. The bag is full and the electrical cord is frayed to the point you take your life in your own hands when you plug it in. The other is the supermodern model that weighs about two-pounds, is as thin as a broom handle and sucks up nothing. The broom is no better. It's the $2.99 model with the plastic handle and plastic, stiff, yellow bristles that sweep up nothing. This broom serves only as an instrument by which the dirt is simply rearranged on the floor. The dust bunnies simply fly over the top of the broom and land at your feet or blow behind you. The mop isn't much more than a wooden pole with frayed strands of dirty rope hanging from it. Am I supposed to wash the floor with this or is this really a prop someone stole from Theatre-by-the-Sea on Route One?

Grilling

I enjoy grilling out when I'm on vacation but I hesitate to use the grill that's in the back of the cottage. I don't think anyone has ever cleaned the grate that you put the food on. There are pieces of the last 100 cookouts stuck to it. The black, charred chunks all look the same but each has its own identity. One was once part of a hotdog, another got separated from the rest of the hamburger and there are probably a few pieces of pork, steak, chicken and fresh-caught fish. I am sure that all of the previous users of this grill used fresh meat, cooked it to perfection and enjoyed it so there is really nothing stuck to the grate that is harmful or that hot coals won't sterilize. Still, I am leery. Perhaps the solution is that each new renter should go to Wal-Mart or Benny's and buy a new grate for about $20.00, use it for two weeks and put it in the trash when they check out. If you don't want to spend the $20.00, simply go to the trash and retrieve the previous renter's grate. Remember, it will be there until Tuesday.

Fix It Now!

Over the years, there have been three or four occasions where relatives or friends have experienced a water, plumbing or electrical problem in the cottage. This is understandable. If it can happen in your own home it can certainly happen at a cottage. However, when it happens in our own home we simply call the plumber or electrician and within hours the problem is fixed. Not so when it happens at a cottage. Renters must notify the realty company, who in turn notify the owner. More often than not, however, the owner cannot be reached. My brother, his wife and their two small children once suffered through three days of no hot water. The owner was made aware of the problem the first day it presented itself but suggested they "wait to see if it straightens itself out." The solution is quite simple. Each cottage owner should be required to carry a pager 24-hours-a-day so they can be reached at anytime by a realtor or a renter. If the problem is not fixed that day the renter should be given double his rent back for that day. If the cottage costs $150 per day to rent, the renter is entitled to $300 for a day's worth of inconvenience. If the problem is not taken care of by the second day, the week is rent-free. If this suggestion were made law you would have cottage owners drawing your bath for you!

Random Rantings

Whose idea was it to provide each cottage with just one recycling bin into which we are to put empty beer and softdrink cans and bottles? I am on vacation. Where am I supposed to put the empties the second hour I'm here?

I have yet to rent an air-conditioned cottage. Even with open windows the night air is still and muggy making sleep next to impossible. A fan in each bedroom would be a godsend. They can be found at Wal-Mart for $19.95. I highly doubt a renter would steal a fan from a cottage since all a cottage owner need do is take inventory on checkout day to determine if any pilferage has taken place. As a renter, the cost of the fan is not the issue. I just don't have enough room in the car to transport one let alone two or three. And if the truth be known, I would gladly go to Wal-Mart and purchase fans for the cottage if I could be assured the owner would see to it the fans would be there next year.

It is Saturday, my first day of vacation and the thought crosses my mind, "Who paid for the cottage today, me or the guy who just checked out?" My rental agreement dates are August 1 to August 14. I assume his dates were July 18 to August 1. So who wound up paying for today, the 1st?

There are several possible answers. He was not charged for today because he had to move out, so I paid. I was not charged because I did not get a full day's use out of the cottage and since he woke up here today, he paid. We each paid for a half day. Or, most likely, we each paid for a *full* day. Not that it matters.

Have you ever made toast in the cottage's 20-year-old toaster? I make the same mistake with the toaster every year. It is never where I want it so I move it. As soon as I pick it up the bottom flap opens releasing all of the crumbs that have accumulated since I cleaned it *last* year.

Although I am grateful my cottage has a microwave oven in which I can defrost frozen foods, I could easily do without it. If there is anything I need thawed within minutes all I need to do is put it in the refrigerator freezer. My ice cream, ice cubes and unfrozen pizzas are a testament to this.

Why does my refrigerator tilt to the right? One of life's minor annoyances is opening the refrigerator door, then reaching into the refrigerator with both hands to get something out only to have the door hit you in the shoulder. Even more aggravating is opening the refrigerator door, then grabbing something off the counter that needs to be refrigerated, only to discover the door has closed before you could get back.

There are some interesting observations to be made as you put food into the refrigerator just after you arrive. Why is there two inches of rusty water in the vegetable bin? And did that mold build up between the time the last family checked out and we checked in?

Opening the freezer for the first time is also an annual adventure. What made the previous renters think I wanted their last two lemon Freezy- Pops still in the box that once contained 12?

Why is it every year I have to go out and buy a corkscrew that works and a bottle opener that's not caked with rust or doesn't have some sticky stuff at the tip? Add matches to the list and a can opener for things like Spaghettios, tuna and baked beans. The 30-year-old metal, dull opener in the cottage barely pierces the can and turning the handle on the rusted implement is impossible.

I always wind up cleaning up something the previous renter neglected to clean. It is something the cottage owner didn't see during her quick cottage check when the last people checked out. I'm the kind of person who figures, "If I don't clean it up, the owner will discover it when I check out and blame it on *me*." So, I clean it.

Most cottages are fairly old and could use electrical updating. One 60-watt bulb in the ceiling is hardly enough to light an entire living room.

If the cottage rental agreement states that the cottage has a television it should be incumbent upon the cottage owner to see that the television actually works, i.e.

that the television can actually receive local channels. The rabbit ears don't do a thing and no configuration of twisted-together wire coat hangers works. If cable TV is one of the perks of the cottage, cottage owners should leave specific instructions as to which buttons to press on which of the three remote controls.

There. I've vented and ranted. I feel so much better. I'm going for a walk on the beach.

Personal Piss Off Crafts

Their correct name is Personal Watercrafts. I call them Personal Piss Off Crafts. I am referring to jet skis, the maritime menace of the new millennium. Westerly would do well to join forces with Weekapaug, Misquamicut and Watch Hill as well as with realtors and cottage owners and ban them. That I am not alone on this issue is evidenced by the growing number of beach communities that have done just that -- banned them.

Have you ever seen a trailer with two jet skis on it parked in the driveway of a cottage? No. And I know why. Vacationing families who pay anywhere from

$800 to $2000 per week for a cottage and spend another $1000 on dining and entertainment *don't bring jet skis* with them!

I find it strange that all jet skiers come out only on weekends. This puzzling situation leads me to one of two conclusions. First, from Monday to Friday jet skiers either stay inside their rented cottages or simply swim in the ocean and only bring their jet skis out on Saturday and Sunday. My second conclusion is that the reason these jet skiers only show up on Saturday and Sunday is because they're *at work* Monday through Friday and they don't rent a cottage at all.

My cottage happens to be located on the Winnapaug Salt Pond on the cove in Weekapaug and is next to a boat landing. The asphalt of the street on which my cottage is located, Winnapaug Ave., leads into the water so boaters can back up their trailers to launch their crafts. Monday through Friday finds this boat landing to be relatively silent with not much activity save for a vacationing (aka cottage renting) family who walks into the water in search of crabs. But on Saturday and Sunday mornings at seven I am jolted out of bed by the sounds of vehicles and people's voices as they guide the drivers of trailers backing up to the water and then the sound of jet ski engines revving up. Along with the noise I can smell the gas and fumes through my bedroom window. I ask myself why, if these 'vacationers' knew they'd be doing some jet skiing on their 'vacation', the smart thing to do would have been to rent a cottage on the water so they could launch off their backyard. Perhaps there wasn't a cottage available on the water that they could rent. Or is it that they don't rent a cottage at all?

After I am jolted from my sleep I decide to get up since there is no sense in trying to go back to sleep with all the noise outside my window. I get dressed and stumble to my car with the intention of going out for the newspaper, coffee and doughnuts. However, I am stopped dead in my tracks at my driveway entrance. I cannot leave because my driveway is blocked by a pickup truck with a trailer hitched to it, backing up to the water's edge to unload two jet skis. My wait will not be a short one either as there are two more vehicles in line wth trailers hitched to them waiting to unload similar cargo. When I am finally able to pull out into the street I realize that Winnapaug Ave. is now a one-lane road. Empty trailers hooked up to pickup trucks line both sides of the street leaving barely enough room for a vehicle to drive through. The trailers are parked snuggly between the 'No Parking' signs that line the street. Apparently the owners of these trailers didn't have enough room to park in the driveways of their *rented cottages*! My return home from my newspaper run finds me once again maneuvering my vehicle down what is now a one-lane Winnapaug Ave. I finally make it into my driveway. As I exit my vehicle and head into the cottage I notice my fellow *renters* are unloading coolers from the backs of their pickup trucks. I assume these coolers are filled with sandwiches that were made earlier in the day at the pickup owners' *rented cottages.* The coolers probably also contain peaches, Cheetos, and cans of Snapple or Coke -- all items taken from the refrigerator at their *rented cottage.* I am sure these coolers couldn't be filled with beer. Jet skiers certainly wouldn't drink alcohol before taking the controls of one of these wave rockets.

Later that day I am faced with much the same scenario when I get to the beach. Noisy, fume-expelling, smoke-belching jet skis zooming parallel to the shoreline. Their speed is such that when they hit even a small swell they become momentarily airborne. Sailboaters, kayakers and people on rafts often find themselves in a state of panic as one of these maritime motorcycles bares down on them only to swerve away at the last second. I dread the thought of one of these machines going out of control and plowing into a group of bathers.

In fairness to the jet skiers, however, perhaps my worries and concerns are unfounded. Certainly these jet ski drivers are extremely careful. After all, their wives and young children will soon be leaving their *rented cottage* to come to the beach to frolic in the waves, won't they?

One Saturday afternoon as my brother Josh and I stood knee-deep in the waves, we sensed a sudden silence. The jet skis had stopped. There was peace. There was quiet. Such relief. Josh remarked, "God, you don't realize just how loud those things are 'til they stop."

Obviously, Westerly Town Fathers et al are convinced that jet skiers and their families actually do rent cottages and contribute heavily to the tourist economy. If they are not convinced then they are knowingly turning a blind eye to a group that pays no rent, uses the roads and boat ramps at no charge, parks illegally for free, blocks traffic, pollutes the air, upsets the aquatic environment and creates havoc for vacationing families who pump millions of dollars into the South County economy each year.

One day in the television newsroom where I work we received a report of a jet ski accident in Michigan. Later that afternoon videotape of the incident arrived in the newsroom. A 23-year-old jet skier turned on the ignition when suddenly, the craft exploded, sending the man skyward as if an ejector-seat button had been pushed. He suffered a broken leg along with cuts and burns but fortunately suffered no serious injury. I took more than just a small amount of pleasure watching the videotape of the burning craft enveloped in smoke as firefighters hosed it down. I thought to myself, "If only all Personal Piss Off Crafts were equipped with a similar ignition."

It's a Fin! I Swear It's a Fin!

You're sitting on your blanket at the beach staring out at the sea and the sailboats, Block Island and the huge freighter that is miles and miles out. Suddenly, you see it. Your eyes are fixed on the spot. It disappears. You rip your sunglasses off and don't dare to blink. You see it again. It's a fin! You swear it's a fin. As you continue to stare you ask yourself, "Is that a shark out there and I'm the only one on the entire beach who knows it?" You want to jump up and start yelling "Shark!" but you have seen the movie *Jaws* and you remember the scene when Amity Police Chief Martin Brody thought he saw a shark, screamed bloody murder and caused a panicked stampede on the beach only to later discover it was a false alarm. You continue your stare, carefully scanning the water's surface where you last saw the fin. Your powers of logic and reason start to take over and you begin to convince yourself that the odds that what you saw is a fin are a million to one. The adrenaline rush subsides and you decide to go back to your book, newspaper or nap after you take just one last glance. There it is! Only this time it has moved 100 yards to the left of its original position. It must be the fin of a shark working its way along the shoreline. You jump to your feet. But just as you do, your 'fin' flaps its wings, skims across the water for a few yards and flies off toward Watch Hill in search of other seagulls just like itself. But rather than be disappointed, you laugh at yourself. You do this every year. You did it last year. You'll do it again next year.

Bactorealiti

A two-week stay in Weekapaug is good not just for the soul but for the body as well. Your hair gets lighter and your skin becomes darker with each day spent under the oceanside sun. You would never say it publicly but after a post- beach shower when your hair is blown dry and combed and you're dressed to go out to dinner it's almost impossible not to say, "Mirror, mirror on the wall, damn I look good!" Not only do you look the best you've looked all year but you're also feeling your best. Breathing the clean ocean air has given new life to your lungs and the salt water has healed every rash, cut and blemish that just wouldn't go away the rest of the year.

Yet, in spite of this healthy lifestyle that has us looking and feeling our best, why is it that on the final day of vacation all husbands and fathers contract the same illness? This illness is borne of a bacteria known as Bactorealiti. I am not a doctor and I don't play one on TV. I am not an expert on the correct pronounciation of this medical term. Thus, my opinion on how to pronounce Bactorealiti is just a layman's guess. But I believe if you were to sound it out it would sound very much like Back To Reality.

The Bactorealiti virus lives and grows inside of every cottage realty office. It is contracted by shaking hands with the realty agent as he says, "See ya next year." The first sign of infection manifests itself as Dad walks out of the realty office having just dropped off the key to the cottage after a two-week vacation. As he gets into the car the family immediately notices he is pale and frowning. He looks as though he has suddenly come down with something. This is the beginning of a year-long bout with Bactorealiti. More symptoms become evident as the car reaches the interstate highway that leads home. Bactorealiti causes a Jeckyll and Hyde transformation. This is the same Dad who, two weeks ago when stuck in bumper-to-bumper beach traffic was relaxed, happy-go-lucky and even lifted the spirits of the rest of the family as they sweltered in the heat and choked on car fumes. Back then his patience knew no bounds. The King of the Clambeds was making his triumphal return to Weekapaug. "Hey, of course there's traffic," he said. "That's because *everybody* wants to get to the beach. But remember, most of these people are just coming for the day. *We're* gonna be here for two weeks! Open the windows! Smell the fresh ocean air. We'll be out of this traffic and at the cottage in no time!"

The ride home finds the King of the Clambeds to be a mere clam shell of his former self. He is silent, withdrawn, somber, depressed and oblivious to the presence of the rest of the family in the vehicle. Yet, while he outwardly appears to be in a catatonic state his mind is racing with a thousand thoughts and emotions that pound his brain like the waves of a storm tide. "I can't believe it's over," he says to himself. "I won't be back here for 351 days. In 48 hours from right now I'll be sitting at my desk at work. The next time I come back here the kids will be a year older. School starts in three weeks. We've gotta get through the kids' school sports activities, band, cheerleading, plays, PTO meetings, Thanksgiving, winter, Christmas, the never-ending cold of January and February, March's muddy mess, taxes, Easter and graduations." All of which he knows will be interspersed with work-related waste-of-time conventions, seminars, projects and meetings.

Bactorealiti is in its most potent state in the six days following the initial infection at the realty office. The condition is exacerbated by the sight of beach sand on the floor and seats of the car as one sits in morning rush hour traffic. During these six critical days Bactorealiti also effects one's concentration. A Wednesday morning meeting finds the sufferer a thousand miles away (or however many miles it is from the office to the cottage) lamenting the fact that, "Last week at this time I was on the front porch of the cottage with *The Hartford Courant* (or *The Boston Globe, The New York Times, The New York Daily News, The Westerly Sun*) and a cup of coffee."

Friday evening, as the Bactorealiti victim walks behind the lawnmower to attack a month's worth of growth and neglect he thinks back to the previous Friday night when he and his wife were sitting on the deck of the Watch Hill Inn nursing cocktails and waiting for the lobster in drawn butter to arrive at the table. Tonight's supper will be spaghetti with Ragu sauce and garlic bread.

After six days the effects of Bactorealiti begin to wear off. Make no mistake -- the affliction still exists within the system but it is now in a dormant state.

Complete recovery comes in 351 days and ironically, the cure is found in the same place where the disease was first contracted -- the cottage realty office.

The View From The Blanket The exact moment of complete recuperation is when the realty agent shakes Dad's hand and asks, "Did you have a good year?" Dad responds, "Oh yeah, no complaints at all." But deep inside, as he accepts the cottage key from the realty agent, he is saying, "I had a great year...and it's about to get a whole lot better."

Welcome home, Oh King of the Clambeds.

TWELVE FOOT thresher shark discovered by Miss JoAnne Zalaski, Terryville near Rhode Island bathing beach.

Terryville

Terryville Correspondent is
J. Francis Ryan
8 Oak Street, Tel. 582-4783

400 Pound Shark Reported By Terryville Girl

The next time daughter JoAnne shouts, "Shark!" Joseph Zalaski of Laurel Avenue, Terryville, will believe it.

The last time was August 9 at the Dunes Park Beach and Seaside Beach Club in Misquamicut, R.I. and Zalaski didn't believe it—at first.

He looked and saw this great tail protruding from the sea about 300 feet offshore. "Its tail was so big it looked like a tentacle from a sea monster," Zalaski said afterward.

A lifeguard was notified and the area was cleared of swimmers.

Then, a lifeguard and a police officer launched a boat and set out to capture a big fish.

Officer Samuel Cilino wounded the shark with eight shots from his service revolver and Lifeguard Bill Friend followed this up with a harpoon from a spear gun.

The shark, which turned out to be a thresher shark about 12 feet long and weighing about 400 pounds, was taken in tow, still thrashing around, and brought ashore.

Another bullet and finally disemboweling were necessary to kill the ugly creature.

It was found to have a big cut on the body apparently from being struck by a boat propellor.

Zalaski, a guidance counselor at Bloomfield High School, theorizes that the shark may have come inshore to excape being cannibalized by some of its own kind attracted by the wound.

He did some checking and found that thrasher sharks may grow as big as 1,000 pounds and 20 feet long. They get their name from an extremely large upper tail fin which is used to sweep foot into their gaping mouths.

Shark!

Anyone who believes that the quaint, protected, idyllic Weekapaug beaches are immune to the dangers of the deep may not want to know what happened on that hot August afternoon in 1967 off the beach next to the Seaside Club near the Weekapaug Breachway. On that day we were visited by not one, but *four* sharks. It was mid-afternoon and I was with my childhood best friend Mark and my cousin Jimmy cruising Atlantic Avenue in Mark's Ford Mustang convertible with the top down. My only memory of our cruise is when Jimmy leaned out of the Mustang's front passenger seat and attempted to grab the buttocks of a binkni-clad girl who was walking along Atlantic Avenue.

As we drove back toward our cottage and approached our beach we saw quite a few people leaving. This was quite unusual as it was a beautiful, cloudless, sunfilled afternoon. Someone shouted to us, "Sharks!" Jimmy and I jumped out of the car and raced up the sand dune toward the beach. Mark was left to park his car back at his family's cottage before he could join in the excitement.

As I walked up over the dune and peered down upon the beach I saw an almost surreal sight. Not a soul was in the water. Everyone on the beach was standing and staring out at the sea. What were they looking at? I then noticed something moving about 200 yards offshore. It was a fin. No, two fins. Three! Four! Four fins! These were not small fins. The tails of these creatures protruded six feet above the ocean surface. I observed three sharks swimming abreast being led by a fourth. They swam back and forth parallel to the beach.

Within minutes a small Coast Guard boat arrived and came close enough to shore to allow a Westerly Police officer to board the craft and head out toward the creatures. When the craft got near the sharks the police officer fired three or four shots in the sharks' direction causing the three followers to head out to sea. The leader, however, remained. A harpoon was fired from the Coast Guard boat and it lodged into the shark. The shark then made a quick, sharp turn and bolted toward shore as onlookers screamed. The boat followed and came ashore. Coast Guard personnel began pulling on the rope attached to the harpoon that was lodged in the shark and after a 20-minute battle the shark was beached. It thrashed, bucked and bolted. Five more shots were fired into its head. It continued to thrash. One of the people on board the Coast Guard boat then slit the shark's stomach open and out came several baby sharks. Soon the shark stopped moving.

The shark was a Thresher shark. It was 12' in length and weighed 400 pounds. There was a large, bleeding gash at the base of its tail. This told the real story of what had just happened at sea. The three sharks that escaped out to sea at the sound of gunshots were not followers, they were predators. This beached shark was not the leader, but rather the 'victim'. The gash in its tail was the result of a run-in with the rudder of a large boat. The blood attracted the other three sharks and the chase was on. It did not end well.

Later that afternoon I learned that my sister Jo-Ann was the first to spot the sharks during a walk on the beach. She ran to our beach screaming at my father, "Shark, shark!" My father had the presence of mind to take pictures of the entire ordeal -- the boat, the gun, the harpoon, the shark thrashing on the beach and the babies flowing out as the shark was cut open. In fact, our local hometown newspaper, *The*

Bristol Press used my father's pictures and interviewed my sister for an article about the incident. The article began with the words, "The next time daughter Jo-Ann shouts, "Shark!" Joseph Zalaski of Laurel Avenue, Terryville, will believe it."

At about 8:00 that night I took a walk on the beach with my cousin and we came upon a sight that sticks in my mind to this day. There was the shark with a big chain wrapped around its tail, hoisted full length in the air on the shovel of a payloader. The shark's body was six-and-a-half-feet long, the tail was another six feet. The animal's liver protruded from its body and measured seven feet. There was a strong smell of iron in the air from the shark's blood.

I walked away wishing the excitement of the day had a happier ending.

The dreaded horsefly!

Horseflies

I've just had a refreshing plunge in the ocean and I am now face-down on my towel. My hair is still wet and dripping. Water beads are rolling down my back, thighs, calves and shoulders. I love this feeling. I somehow think I'm getting a better, deeper, richer tan because the relentless sun is frying the waterbeads onto the surface of my skin. I'm not sleepy but it feels wonderful to close my eyes and rest my head on my folded forearms as I breathe deeply trying to catch my breath from my run out of the waves to my towel.

The tranquility of this perfect moment is broken by a twinge on the back of my calf. It itches, so I lift the opposite foot and scrape it across the offending calf. For a few seconds all is right with the world again until the itch comes back. I convince myself it's simply the sand from the foot that I just scraped across it.

Then comes a new itch. This one is right between my shoulder blades and I can't reach it but I know this is definitely not the result of sand. Now the itch moves to my lower back just above the waistband of my bathing suit. I brush it with my hand and it leaves temporarily.

Logic tells me that all of these itches are simply the result of water and salt drying on my skin. But logic be damned. I know that any one of these innocent itches could be a dreaded horsefly!

I call them horseflies. Some people call them deer flies. No matter what you call them they are a sunbather's nightmare. They are much bigger than the flies you have at your house. They are thick and fat as if on steroids. Their eyes and heads are a bright, menacing green as if they're wearing goggles to help them zero in on you. Their bite is horrendous. You'd rather suffer through a shot of cortisone or novocaine.

There is no greater satisfaction than killing one of these creatures. However, to do so involves a complicated strategy. If this green-eyed monster lands on your wife , husband or child, the only thing you can do is shoo it off the person. You can't slap it. The force required to subdue this beast would knock the wind out of someone, perhaps even break a bone or at the very least draw blood. So you must wait until the horsefly lands on you and you must either be sitting up straight or standing to enhance your chances of a successful swat.

Finally, the moment of truth arrives. The horsefly has landed on your forearm and you can smell victory. You slowly raise your opposite hand and position it over the unsuspecting insect at which point panic sets in as you say to yourself, "Is he gonna bite me before I swat him?" Then WHAM! Your hand comes down so hard and so fast that you unwittingly inflict pain upon yourself. Your first indication of success comes a split second after the swat as you look at your forearm and see a small spot of what looks like green ink. You did something -- you're just not sure what. Your eyes immediately scan the area around your feet and suddenly you see something dark lying in the white sand. You got him! But even now you're not thrilled about picking him up. We somehow have it in our head that even a dead horsefly can hurt us. So we gingerly pick it up by one of its wings and thus begins our victory lap. We show it to anyone and everyone around us and we enhance the feeling of conquest by saying, "Oh God, can you imagine if this thing bit one of the kids?"

You dodged the bullet this time. But there will be another day and another horsefly. Deep down inside you know that without at least one bite per year it just wouldn't be the beach, would it?

Sand Shaking Etiquette

The true test to determine if someone is a seasoned beach veteran or a novice to the nuances of beach culture is to observe the way that one shakes sand from a towel or blanket. There are certain rules of etiquette to be followed and anyone who violates these rules invites the wrath of those of us schooled in proper sandshaking procedure.

Even on a nice, hot, sunny beach day novices usually leave the beach before the veterans do. Thus, a novice's sandshaking transgressions are carried out in full view of, and suffered by those who know better. It is much like the culturally-challenged buffoon who goes to the opera and doesn't turn his cellphone off.

The novice who has had his fill of sun and surf for the day acts as if he is the only person on the beach. He is oblivious to those around him. He picks up his wet, sand-caked towel, closes his eyes, holds his breath, turns his head sideways and shakes the towel violently. Everyone around him is just as violently shaken as the sudden sandstorm jolts them from their towels and blankets. Sand is everywhere. It is in your eyes, your mouth, it stings your face, coats your sandwich and gets into your can of soda. You have an overwhelming urge to grab the novice by the neck or at the very least let loose with an expletive shouted on behalf of all of your fellow violated veterans.

The veteran sandshaker does not pick his towel up from the ground. Rather, he grasps one end of it and gently drags it along the sand toward the water's edge. The super-considerate veteran will even bend his knees, crouch down and stay low to the ground so as not to let the wind catch any portion of the towel. Once at the water's edge the veteran will pick up the towel, wade knee-deep into the surf, check to see that no bathers are near and shakes the towel to his satisfaction. As the veteran properly executes this procedure he knows appreciative eyes are upon him. His reward is knowing that non-verbally he has told the entire beach, "I am a beach veteran." He now maneuvers through towels, blankets and bodies as he makes his exit.

With an air of confidence he silently says to himself, "Novices take notice. We have drawn a line in the sand."

Parking

Whatever was left of the laid back lure of the vacation atmosphere at the restaurants, bars, shops and attractions along Atlantic Avenue died the year they began to 'hawk' parking. Every patch of dirt, sand, pebbles or tall grass that doesn't have a building on it is now a parking lot. Alleyways, mudpuddles, grassy fields and any space behind restaurant dumpsters all qualify. Restaurant. Parking lot. Ice cream stand. Parking lot. Miniature golf course. Parking lot. Go-Karts. Parking lot. Beach bar. Parking lot. Batting cages. Parking lot. Waterslide. Parking lot. Convenience store. Parking lot.

These so-called parking lots are easy to spot. Your first clue is the plywood sign pounded into the ground that says 'Parking' and looks as though some six- year-old painted the letters. If you've ever seen a B-western on Saturday afternoon TV and the hero cowboy rides up to a sign that says "Dead Man's Gulch," then you know what these parking signs look like. On weekdays they drag out the sign that says "Parking $5." On Saturday and Sunday mornings out comes the "Parking $10" sign. At 10 A.M. the signs say, "Parking $20". At about 2 o'clock on weekend afternoons when business begins to slow down it's fire sale time and they bring out their "Parking $8" sign.

Next to the sign you will find one of two types of people. First is the college kid who wants a summer job but not a real job where you'd have to punch a clock, produce something or answer to a boss. The attire for college *girls* consists of a bathing suit top and frayed shorts. They are blonde, tanned, and talk and act like the airhead cheerleader you pray your daughter will never become.

The college *guys* take it a step further. This is their big chance to act like the Rent-A-Cop at the mall and they play the role to the hilt. They dress in bright orange bathing suits much like the local lifeguard who actually has some degree of authority. Their blond hair and tans are accentuated when contrasted with the huge glob of white zinc oxide on their noses. They wear reflective sunglasses so you can't see their eyes making them look very much like a state police officer or a prison guard on a chain gang in Texas.

The other type of person you'll see is the 40 to 55-year old beach bum who looks like a cross between singer Jimmy Buffet and comedian Gallagher. They are balding, their faces and skin show the effects of too many summers in the sun and they seem to know everyone on the entire street. They don't remember their last real job and they dread their next one when summer ends.

Regardless of which type of person you see, whether it be the college kid or the aging hippie, they're both doing the same thing -- motioning you to pull into *their* parking lot.

You almost feel guilty for *not* pulling in to the point that you feel obligated to roll down your window and explain that you have a cottage and you're just going to church, to breakfast or to Watch Hill.

The only time you are forced to deal with one of these asphalt Adonis' is when you and your family attempt to patronize a seaside establishment for lunch, a snack or a cold drink. As you enter the parking lot you roll down your window because you see Jimmy Buffet or Norman Noxema approaching. Without so much as a "hello," "welcome," or "Good afternoon, where are you going?" the attendant leans into your window, shoves his hand in front of your face and says, "That's

$10." The $10 fee is what one would pay to park in the lot and spend the day on the beach. Restaurant patrons park free. You are now about to be subjected to the ultimate insult. This parking lot flunky who is making minimum wage will now play judge and jury as you try to convince him that you're really going to the restaurant and not the beach. He acts as though he believes your story and points you toward the restaurant parking area. However, if you look in your rear view mirror, you will notice that the attendant and two others are watching you like hawks. They stare you down as you and your family get out of the car and their eyes don't leave you until the restaurant door closes behind you.

A Sight To Behold

Blind Girl

It was one of those perfectly clear days on the beach. You could see for miles in all directions. There was no fog, no haze, no mist, no clouds, no anything except a blue sky made bluer by the bright sunshine.

As my brother Matthew and I sat in our lounge chairs on our beach in Weekapaug we marveled at the clarity of the day. Watch Hill was six miles to the right of our position yet we commented that the Ocean House and the Watch Hill Coast Guard Lighthouse looked as though they were just 100 yards up the beach. The water glistened as the sun beat down upon it. We could see right through each shining wave as it broke toward shore. This was the day we dreamed about when we were shoveling two feet of snow from our January driveways. Today, the dream was a reality.

I gazed once again to my right toward Watch Hill and I focused on the Ocean House knowing that later that afternoon I would be relaxing on the outdoor porch of that grand hotel enjoying a beverage, the ambiance and the view.

But my idyllic gaze was interrupted by something just 30 feet to my right. There sat a blind girl. She looked to be about 25 and was sitting on a folding beach chair. She wore bluejean shorts and a yellow, short-sleeved top. Her hair was shoulder length, dark and curly. Near her chair was a blue beach blanket occupied by two older women whom I guessed were her mother and perhaps an aunt. I could not account for the two young children with them. The two older women chatted. The children played in the sand.

The blind girl sat there, eyes wide open, staring blankly, moving her gaze in the direction of any sound or voice within her auditory range.

I am not blind so I don't pretend to have any special insight into what this young lady's mind's eye was seeing. The closest I could come to putting myself in her place was to remember those times when I flopped down on my towel, face down and eyes closed after an exhilirating beating in the waves. The beach becomes a very different, even strange place from this position.

I hear footsteps near my towel and someone kicks up a light dusting of sand that hits the back of my thighs. Is it one of my nieces, nephews, brothers or sisters -- or is it a stranger? I hear a father shout, "Jimmy, that's *his* pail, give it back to him." I hear screaming followed by the sound of the crash of a huge wave. Did someone get hurt or were they just excited about getting caught in the wave? I hear a conversation coming from a nearby blanket -- "We went up to Narragansett last night and ate at the Coast Guard House Restaurant. The food was....". The wind kicks up and drowns out the end of the sentence denying me a critique of the restaurant's cuisine. At another nearby blanket someone with a boombox is looking for a radio station they like. In the process they stop momentarily at a station where the announcer intones, "And at Fenway Park today where the Red Sox played host to the Yankees...." Before I can hear the all-important score (which, in reality, won't change my life one iota!) the person changes the station.

What separates me from the blind girl is that any time I want I can pop up off my towel, open my eyes, focus and see the kid with the pail. I can look at the people who were talking about the Coast Guard House and if I'm really into baseball I can walk up to anyone on the beach who has a radio and ask about the Red Sox score.

I got up from my towel and took a walk on the beach in the direction of the Misquamicut State Beach and Watch Hill. I walked for perhaps 10 minutes and turned back. When I was approximately 100 yards away from my towel I saw the blind girl and one of the older women arm-in-arm walking toward me. As I got closer to them the older woman picked up a rock about the size of an apple and placed it in the blind girl's hand. The girl clasped the rock tightly in both hands and while I could not hear the conversation I was sure the older woman was describing the color and was asking her young companion if she could feel the shape and coolness of the object.

I got back to my towel, sat down and looked out at the ocean. I thought to myself that we should all, at least once a day pick up a rock, tightly press our hands together around it and close our eyes. We should then drop the rock, keep our hands pressed tightly together, open our eyes, look skyward and say, "Thank You."

The stairs Uncle John ascended with the child's lifeless body

Drowning

I am glad I wasn't on the beach that horrible day. It wasn't until late that afternoon that my cousin told me what had happened.

It was the summer of '64 give or take a year. I was 11 or 12 years old. Instead of spending the day on the beach I was six miles out to sea aboard the charter fishing boat *Bobby-D* out of Watch Hill. We would rent the *Bobby-D* twice each summer and on that particular day it was my turn to be part of the maximum capacity party of six that included my father, grandmother, grandfather, uncle and one of my brothers. After six hours on the high seas we headed into port with an impressive catch of flatfish, flounder and sea bass which my grandmother would filet and prepare for that evening's meal. My father paid the boat captain the $25 fee and tipped him another $2 for tangled lines and for baiting children's hooks.

When we arrived back at our cottage the entire street was abuzz with what had happened. A little boy drowned off our beach that afternoon. He was seven years old. They found him floating in 10 feet of water. We learned his family had come just for the day. They were visiting friends who had a cottage. I was also told that my Uncle John Krinitsky who was chief of police in our hometown of Terryville, Connecticut played a role in the day's events. Uncle John and his family rented a cottage for two weeks each year, so on that day, he was on the beach doing what most vacationing parents do -- reading, soaking up the sun and watching his children.

When the little boy's body was found, Uncle John identified himself as a law officer. No one was about to question the authority of this 6'3" man with a dark complexion and jet black hair. In fact, these bystanders were probably grateful that someone stepped forward to take charge of such a distasteful situation. Uncle John carried the child's lifeless body up some steep wooden, weather-beaten steps and into a cottage that sat atop a dune next to our beach. I did not need to hear that the boy's mother, in her shock and grief, was unable to stand and had to be carried off the beach.

I wasn't there that day but I have a pretty good idea of what it was like. The child's parents were on the beach chatting with the friends they were visiting. Every few minutes Mom or Dad would scan the water's edge to make sure their child was in sight. But an undertow or riptide doesn't take a few minutes. It takes only seconds to pull even an adult underwater and suck him 100 yards out to sea before releasing its grip. This 100-yard underwater ordeal is like being tumbled in a clothes dryer full of water. One's natural instinct is to fight it. But the more one fights the more one loses energy and oxygen. The ocean wins the fight and the victim's waterlogged body descends to the ocean floor. When the sea decides to give it up the body rises to the surface and floats.

There is no way the parents could ever have known their child was in trouble. There is no such thing as a cry for help in the rough Atlantic Ocean. No one can hear you. The beach is crowded with people listening to radios, throwing footballs, running and laughing. The wind is blowing and kicking up sand. The waves are pounding to the point you can barely hear the person next to you. A child's cry for help would be futile.

I can hear the child's mother asking her husband, "Bob, do you see Jimmy? I don't see him." Bob scans the water's edge where he last saw his son and turns to his hosts. "Do you see him?" In unison the four adults stand up at their blanket and begin staring at every child in the water. No one sees Jimmy at which point the mother begins calling out, "Jimmy!" There will be no answer. The father imitates the call only louder. The father's call sounds angry but it is fear and panic disguised as manly bravado. There will be no answer. The four walk quickly toward the water's edge. As they pace frantically parallel to the waves the mother pleads with her husband, "Bob, where is he?!" She follows with the first of many screams of "Jimmy!" One of their hosts runs to get a lifeguard. By this time everyone on the beach is aware that something is very wrong. Two women run up to the mother and ask, "What does he look like?" "What was he wearing?" Parents jump from their blankets and order their children out of the water as if a shark has been sighted. The mother continues to scream her son's name. The father and four or five other men are waist-deep in the waves searching. The rest of the people on the beach are standing in silence. They shudder with each new piercing, frantic, helpless scream from the boy's mother.

A lifeguard shows up. A small boat patrols the waters 300 yards off shore. It doesn't help the boy's parents to see a diver jump from the boat and into the water. Some people leave the beach to avoid the sheer horror of the situation.

The View From The Blanket Others leave out of respect for the family knowing realistically there is nothing that can be done. Those who remain will hear one more blood-curdling shriek from the mother when the body is discovered and brought to shore. It is a shriek that pierces the silence of the beach. It is a shriek that will haunt everyone who heard it.

Nearly 40 years later I sometimes think of those parents. If they are still alive they are 65 to 70 years old. For 40 years they have lived with the nightmare of that day. They have no doubt wondered what Jimmy, who would be nearly 50, would be like today. I wonder what their relationship has been all these years with the friends who invited them to the cottage for the day. I am sure the parents have never gone back to that beach.

It is a sad irony that the very spot that I have called Heaven for the past 40 years has been just the opposite for someone else.

Children crabbing at the Weekapaug Breachway

Crabbing With A Drop Line

Crabbing with a drop line is the ultimate experience in touching, feeling and coexisting with ancient sea life. A father who takes his children crabbing knows that his kids are *definitely* going to catch *something!* It's impossible not to.

A drop-line is simply a thick piece of string with a large sinker at the end of it. All one need do is tie a fish head or fish carcass with the string, drop the line in the water and crabs will crawl all over themselves trying to latch on to what to a crab is a sweet-smelling meal.

An army of crabs ranging in size from miniscule to monstrous will latch onto the bait. When the child pulls the drop line up out of the water most of the crabs will let go of the bait and drop off. Some will hang on for dear life. And there will always be that one, huge, dark crab that tenaciously hangs on. As this crab is pulled up out of the water it still hangs on. It doesn't care that it has been ripped out of its ocean environment and is now in midair. This crab will hang onto its prey at any cost.

This crab suddenly finds itself dipped into a plastic red pail filled with water. The bait is jerked away from the creature and the crab is left to wallow in a clear bucket of sea water. He moves in a circle along the bottom of the pail looking for a way out. He vainly tries to climb up the slippery side of the pail. Within minutes another crab that has met the same fate joins him. They grab onto each other, each believing the other is that beautiful piece of fish head that got jerked away.

The nice part about a crabbing experience is that everybody wins -- Dad, the kids and the crabs. Dad is happy because his kids caught some crabs and put them in their buckets. The kids are happy because they caught some crabs and got to bring them home. The crabs are happy because once back at the cottage, Dads always say to their kids, "Let's throw 'em back in the bay and catch 'em tomorrow." There is no greater pleasure than watching your children dump a pail of crabs out and then watching the crabs fan out across the ocean bottom to freedom.

Seaweed poppers that grow on the rocks in the Weekapaug Breachway

Seaweed Poppers

There are certain experiences in life we never get tired of or outgrow no matter how old we are. Seeing Santa Claus on a float in a Christmas parade will always excite us whether we're nine or 90. Will you ever outgrow lying in bed and having someone unfurl a blanket over your head allowing it to float gently down over your body? You want them to do it over and over again as if you were five years old. High on my list is the ecstasy of looking into the bottom of the cup of my nearly finished hot fudge sundae and realizing that there are four spoonsful of pure hot fudge left. I also have a juvenile fascination with opening all the drawers in my hotel room to check out the stationery, postcards, pens and little note pads the hotel has provided.

Such is the case with seaweed poppers. I am sure this is not their correct name but it's what I call them -- the seaweed that has the squeezable rubbery balls at the end. This seaweed attaches itself to rocks along the shoreline or breachway and moves back and forth with the ebb and flow of the tide.

Grabbing a fistful of seaweed poppers and tearing them from the rocks to which they are attached is no easy task. One must first make the treacherous climb down the steep rock formation that leads into the breachway's waters. The rocks at the water's edge that have the seaweed poppers attached to them are covered with green moss and some unknown substance that's black and slippery. One false step and your feet fly out from under you causing you to either fall backward onto the rocks or forward into the breachway. So you carefully plant your feet and use one hand to grab onto a nearby rock to steady yourself. You now stretch toward the water as far as you dare. Your free hand reaches into the water to grab and pull a large bunch of seaweed poppers. Do not claim victory just yet, though!

You now have to negotiate the steep rock climb upward, a journey made all the more difficult by the fact that you now have just one free hand with which to hang on to the rocks to balance yourself -- the other hand is full of seaweed poppers. Once on terra firma, the fun begins. You place a seaweed popper between your thumb and forefinger and squeeze. Not only does the popper emit a 'pop' but you are also treated to a light spray of salt water on your face. The nice part is that as you squeeze you can look directly at each popper without fear. You can't do that when you pop a balloon. When I pop a morning-after party balloon by squeezing it or jabbing it with a knife I do it with a certain degree of fear and discomfort. I turn my head. I grimace. I treat the balloon as if it were a hand grenade or a stick of dynamite that is somehow going to hurt me.

After squeezing 10 or 12 poppers I'm satisfied for another year. I toss the spent batch of poppers into the breachway and watch it disappear in whatever direction the tide is flowing.

Do I feel badly that I just killed some kelp simply for my personal amusement? No. My batch of seaweed will soon wash ashore, dry out, breakdown and make its way back into the sea to serve as the nutrients that will help another batch of seaweed poppers grow.

Perhaps the very batch I'll pop next year.

A miniature golfer's worst nightmare!

Miniature Golf

One of the great, time-honored family beach experiences is a night out at the miniature golf range. Miniature golf is not something one puts on the 'must do' vacation itinerary -- it just seems to happen. The origins of the excursion can be traced to a conversation beneath a beach umbrella earlier that day. Mom picks her head up from her book, Dad sets the *New York Times* in his lap and as they both stare out to sea after checking on the kids one of them says, "What do you want to do tonight?" The conversation goes as follows:

Mom: "The kids are gonna be hungry when we get back to the cottage. I've got pasta shells and spaghetti sauce already made and we've got that loaf of garlic bread so we don't have to worry about supper."

Dad: "I told Billy I'd take him on the Go-Karts one of these nights." Mom: "The girls don't wanna do Go-Karts."

Dad: "OK, so what do we do? I don't wanna sit in a movie theater." Mom: "What about miniature golf? The kids love that and we'll be back pretty early."

Dad: "Maybe after that we can get 'em settled in and we can go up to Paddy's for one or two."

Thus, the night is etched in stone. A quick pasta and garlic bread supper, miniature golf, bring the kids home and Mom and Dad get to go out for a couple of drinks. Vacation perfection.

The attire for an evening of miniature golf defies logic. Nights at the beach are cool and damp. Although the calendar might say it's late July or early August, 'chilly' is the word used most often by those who venture out into the seaside evening air. Everyone dons their thickest sweaters. Mom and the girls may even add a hooded parka into the mix. Dad and the boys are, at the very least, wearing their Old Navy or Abercrombie & Fitch windbreakers. Yet, they're all wearing *shorts* and tennis shoes with no socks! This makes about as much sense as the guy who goes to McDonalds and orders two Big Macs and a large fry but opts for a *Diet* Coke because he's watching his weight.

Finding a parking space in the lot next to the miniature golf course is never a problem. There is only your car and two others. The parking lots across the street however, are jam packed with the cars of people who are inside the warm and cozy seaside bars and restaurants enjoying Long Island Iced Tea along with lobster and shrimp cocktail. You try to take some solace by telling yourself that the reason you are not in one of those cozy bars or restaurants is because you're a good parent doing something with the kids. It's not working.

The guy who is manning the miniature golf 'hut' has had his eye on you from the moment you got out of your car. He has already counted the number of people in your party and figured out which ones were 12 or under so by the time you get to the window of the hut he already has the proper number of clubs and balls laid out on the counter plus the scorecard and pencil. He will not so much as say, "Hello," "Good evening," "Hope you have a good time," or even "Here on vacation?" The only thing he does say is, "$13.75." You politely *hand* him a $20 bill only to have $6.25 in change shoved back at you across the countertop. As you stuff the change into your shorts you reward his rudeness with a "Thank you." You're thinking, "Oh what the hell. The poor guy's 60 years old stuck working in a miniature golf hut on a nice summer night." Don't feel too sorry for him. He's the owner. He'll collect enough $13.75's in three summer months to allow him to play real golf in Florida for the next nine months while you're putting in 60-hour work weeks. There is a cruel irony in the fact that while the word "putting" is spelled just one way, it has *two* pronounciations and *two* very different connotations. You are at work *putting* in a long week. He is in Florida, club in hand, *putting* on the 4th green.

The first hole at every miniature golf range is designed to be a confidence- builder for all players regardless of age or skill level. It is usually a 20-foot straight shot toward a hole with no obstacles. Veterans of the Miniature Golf Tour can easily predict what will happen when Mom, Dad and two kids play the hole. Mom goes first. She bounces the ball lightly off the back wall, and the ball lands within one foot of the hole. Little Billy is next and his shot bounces harder off the wall, careens off another wall and sits in the corner four feet away from the hole. Sister Sally is next. She strokes the ball evenly and the bounce off the back wall sees the ball roll right into the cup for a hole-in-one. Dad is the last to hit. He bangs the ball off the back wall in hopes of making a straight landing into the cup. However, Dad's shot is too hard. It caroms off the wall, skips over the hole and rolls back toward the tee. Dad, disappointed, prepares to catch the ball, much like a New York Yankee third baseman would field a ground ball. The only problem is Dad is not a New York Yankee third baseman, he doesn't have a baseball glove and the ball is one-quarter the size of a baseball. Thus, the result is predictable. Just as Dad bends down to snatch the errant shot the ball hits the edge of the square rubber pad he teed off from, the ball bounces over his hand, past his sockless ankles and rolls toward the hut. After a short chase Dad grabs the ball and stands straight up again only to find himself at the hut window face-to-face with hut guy. Hut guy looks up from his *National Enquirer* and gives Dad a look that says, "Why am I not surprised?"

Things go a bit more smoothly for the next three or four holes. The scorecard has everyone shooting a three, a four and an occasional six. The real trouble starts at hole number six -- the dreaded lighthouse! You have to hit the ball under the lighthouse and toward the hole on the other side. But unless you hit the ball directly down the middle of the astroturf carpet and under the very center of the lighthouse you will hear the sound that every miniature golfer dreads -- THUD! Your ball hits something under the lighthouse and does not come out the other side like everyone else's ball did. Although it is not Dad's ball, Dad, being a good Dad lies flat on his stomach on the astroturf fairway and pokes his putter under the lighthouse in an attempt to push the ball out the other side. As fate would have it, at that very moment, hut guy walks past on his way to replacing a burned out lightbulb in the string of lights that hangs over the entire course. Hut guy looks down at the prone figure on the astroturf fairway. Dad sheepishly looks up at hut guy. The look on hut guy's face says, "Oh, you again. Why am I not surprised?"

Somewhere around the ninth hole you realize there is a young couple playing behind you. Since there are four of you and just two of them you offer to let them go ahead of you. They politely decline with a "Oh thanks, but we're in no hurry." Four holes later, after your foursome has registered a series of 11's on your scorecards you notice the couple behind you is no longer behind you. You see them in the parking lot walking toward their car. They didn't quit while they were ahead. They quit because *you* were ahead of them. They headed to the warm and cozy seaside bars and restaurants enjoying Long Island Iced Tea along with lobster and shrimp cocktail. You try to take some solace.

Hole number 16 runs along the chain link fence that separates the golf course from the sidewalk and road. To successfully negotiate this hole one must hit the ball up and around a large, metal loop. The ball must be hit hard enough to maintain centrifugal force on its journey up, around and down the loop and toward the hole.

Your foursome studies the obstacle and comes to the conclusion that each player will have to hit the ball with 'determined authority,' sometimes pronounced 'hard,' if the loop is to be conquered. It is almost a certainty that one member of your foursome will hit the ball *so* hard that it immediately becomes airborne off the tee as if whacked with a three wood instead of a putter. The ball begins a wild adventure. First, it caroms off the metal loop or a nearby lightpost and takes a hard bounce on the black asphalt pathway that connects each hole. The ball then bounces *over* the fence, takes another bounce on the concrete sidewalk and rolls into the street. Fortunately for you, a 20-something guy and his girlfriend who are walking down the sidewalk see the ball bounce in front of them and their eyes follow it into the street. The guy is dressed like the cool beach guy Dad always wanted to be but never quite made it. This young, slender, chiseled young man looks like he just stepped out of an Abercrombie & Fitch catalog. He checks the traffic in both directions, darts out into the street and retrieves the ball. As he walks toward the sidewalk he tosses the ball underhanded over the fence where Dad makes a valiant, but unsuccessful attempt to catch it. The young couple hears Dad's feeble and sheepish 'thank you.' What they didn't hear were the words Dad *really* wanted to say -- "*I know you think I'm the one who hit the ball over the fence and I'm an uncoordinated geek. But it wasn't me! It was one of the kids! Really!*" However, the young couple is already crossing the street, heading toward one of those warm and cozy seaside bars and restaurants to enjoy Long Island Iced Tea along with lobster and shrimp cocktail.

Once you have completed the 18 holes of golf you have the option of playing the bonus hole which could result in winning a free game of golf. This bonus hole looks like a clown's face with a hole in its nose. The player who gets a hole-in-one into the clown's nose wins a free game on the next visit. A winning shot usually triggers a bell or a buzzer and since the bonus hole is located right next to the hut, hut guy knows your foursome is about to turn in your clubs and one of you has won a free game. As you lay the four clubs on the countertop hut guy pulls out a Free Game card and signs and dates it. He slides it across the countertop at you without so much as a "Hope you had fun!", "Hey, who's the lucky one?", "Thanks for coming," or "Hope to see you folks back again some night." Yet, you again reward his rudeness with a "Thank you."

Before you stuff the Free Game card into your pocket, you read it. It says, *This card entitles the holder to one free round of miniature golf at Frank Scungili's Pitch 'n Putt.* On the line that says *Authorized By* you can see that hut guy didn't even bother to sign his full name -- just his initials. F.S.

When you arrive back at the cottage and get the kids settled in, the plan you made earlier in the evening to sneak out for a couple of cocktails seems almost laughable. You've just spent an evening crawling for balls, chasing errant shots, slapping mosquitoes, dodging moths and dealing with hut guy. The thought of driving back to one of those seaside bars and pushing through the crowd for a five-buck beer and a watered-down wine is ludicrous. You open the refrigerator, take five big gulps of iced tea right out of the pitcher and collapse onto the couch. As you shift your body to get comfortable something jabs you in your right buttock. You reach into your back pocket and remove the scorekeeping pencil.

If this empty lot and the clambeds behind it could talk, what story might they tell?

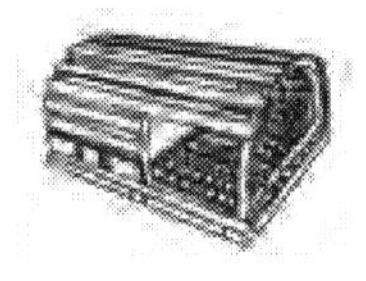

Baci Saw A Murder

Only two people know what happened that night. The killer and Baci. I don't know if the killer ever revealed his dark secret to anyone. Baci kept the secret for some 40 years before telling it to a select few family members who, in turn, imparted the story to me. The journalist in me longs to interview Baci so I could ask her to detail the events of that evening. But alas, Baci left us in 1996, so all I have to go on are family recollections of what she told them.

When Baci finally broke her silence about the incident she was in her late 80's and her memory was not clear as to the exact year it happened. But since her story centers on a cottage that has since been demolished -- a cottage we grandchildren don't remember-- I would guess the year to be somewhere around 1950.

Baci (the Polish word for 'grandmother' and pronounced Botch-ee) and my grandfather would rent the cottage Nan Sea on Breach Drive the last week of July and the first week of August each summer. Behind the Nan Sea and the other cottages on that side of the street were the clambeds and the Winnapaug Salt Pond. The clambeds consisted of a system of narrow, reed-lined tributaries that fed into the salt pond. Some of these sandy-bottomed little rivers were just five feet wide and only ankle deep. Minnows race just ahead of your toes as you wade through the water. Other tributaries were up to 20 feet wide and had water chest-high. At low tide the water level in these tributaries drops dramatically to the point that the smaller tributaries turn simply into mud flats. In the larger tributaries, low tide brings the chest-high waters down to your knees. Low tide was prime time to catch clams. Each change of the tide would bring in a new batch of clams as well as a new layer of sand and silt in which the clams could bury themselves.

That summer, during the two-week time period Baci was in the Nan Sea, the cottage next door was rented by a man, his wife and at least two children and very shortly it became apparent they were not having a good vacation. On more than one occasion when Baci would step outside to hang wet towels and bathing suits on the clothesline she would hear loud, violent arguments coming from the cottage next door. If I know Baci she probably shook her head in disgust, whispered a quick prayer in Polish to St. Somebody and then went inside the cottage and sat in the rocking chair by the window while clutching her rosary beads.

One evening, the all-too-frequent fighting escalated to a level Baci had not heard before. The yelling was louder. The screaming more panicked. There were thuds as if some*thing* or some*one* were being banged around. Then it stopped. There was silence. All was quiet. As Baci sat in the rocking chair reading the newspaper or praying the rosary she periodically glanced out the window and looked toward the next-door-neighbor's cottage. It was during one of these glances that she saw it.

Walking from the back of the cottage next door and toward the clambeds was a man. He was carrying something large and covered. One could surmise he was simply taking out the trash. The only problem with that theory is that cottage trash cans are usually located up against the side of the cottage or just a few feet outside the cottage door. Perhaps he was discarding the entrails of a large fish he had just cleaned. Throwing this theory into question are two things. First, almost everyone who catches and cleans fish either dumps the entrails into the trash cans or takes them to the breachway's deep waters where crabs and other sealife can feast on them. Second, if anyone caught a fish as large as the object the man was carrying, it surely would have been the talk of the street earlier in the day.

When he emerged from the clambeds and walked back to the cottage he no longer had the large object with him. If it was trash or fish entrails that he tossed back there a telltale sign of their location would be hordes of seagulls that would have descended upon the foul-smelling mass the next day. Baci never mentioned seeing any seagulls. Thus, it stands to reason that whatever the man carried into the clambeds, he must have buried deep enough into the soft silt to insure seagulls or crabs would not be attracted to it. With each change of the tide a new layer of sand and silt would cover the object, burying it deeper and deeper. If the sand and silt and changing tides caused the object to settle deeper by just one foot per year simple math tells you how far down it would be some 50 years later.

Baci said she was afraid to notify the police of her suspicions. This was 1950. You minded your own business. So she kept silent. For 40 years.

Indulge me now as I use the absence of documented facts as an excuse to speculate about what happened in the days that followed.

If, in fact, there was a murder, the killer got away with his crime thanks in part to some unwitting accomplices who made any investigation impossible by destroying any evidence. Immediately following the deed the killer no doubt cleaned up the crime scene, making sure any blood was wiped up, the floors were swept and mopped and all disturbed pieces of furniture were put back in place. When checkout day arrived he cleaned the cottage again as all renters are required to do. Then came his first accomplice -- the cleaning service or the owner who came to scour the cottage in preparation for the next renters. Hours later, in came the *next* accomplices -- the next renters. For the next two weeks these new renters and their children sat on the furniture, cleaned fish, shucked clams and dragged in sand, snails and other sea life. When they left they cleaned the cottage as did the cleaning service after them. The cycle went on for weeks so that by summer's end scores of people and several cleanings had wiped out any evidence of a brutal crime.

Meanwhile, the killer is back home, perhaps in Connecticut, New York, or even as far away as Utah and it is days, maybe even weeks before anyone begins to notice that Martha (the name I'll give to our murder victim) hasn't been around much. Finally, the questions do come and the killer feigns embarrassment and he reluctantly admits to family and friends that, "She left me while we were on vacation. She said she needed time for herself and then she'd come back. I have no idea where she went off to." In sympathy, family and friends lend support and comfort to the forlorned and jilted husband.

Even if someone were to eventually become suspicious of the man's story, what could they do? Even if Westerly police were summoned to the cottage to investigate, what could *they* do? Remember, this is 1950. There is no such thing as DNA testing. Evidence gathering was primitive by today's standards. The science had not yet been developed to detect and lift blood spatters or dried blood chips from the hardwood floor or carpet. And even if the woman's fingerprints were found among the thousands of others in the cottage it would merely establish that she had been there -- something the husband certainly would not deny.

If at the time of the murder the couple's two children were somewhere around six or seven years old they were no doubt sleeping or at least in their bedrooms during the yelling, the screaming and the ultimate act. All they knew is that the next day their mother wasn't there. If they are still alive today, those two children would be more than 60 years old. I wonder if they've gone through life believing their mother abandoned them? I wonder if during all these years they've felt sorry for their father whose wife so coldheartedly left him and two children and never came back?

We don't know what really happened that night. The killer's identity and whereabouts are unknown. He may be dead. Baci is gone. The cottage is gone. All that is left is an empty, wild, shrub-filled lot that borders the clam beds.

When the children do pass on I am sure they will be met at Heaven's gate not by St. Peter, but by a 4'11" woman with a noticeable Polish accent grasping a string of rosary beads. She will say to them, "You were not abandoned. Your mother has been here since the day you last saw her. She is very anxious to see you."

A Walk On The Beach

Our family spends all too much of our precious vacation time making plans. We can never simply decide to *do* something and then *do* it! We are the prime example of the too many cooks who don't necessarily spoil the soup but we seem to take forever to cook it.

A case in point is when someone suggests that we all go out to dinner that evening. *Everybody* has to be brought into the decision-making process and it seems as though *everybody* has some sort of scheduling conflict that prevents us from leaving as a group at an agreed upon time to an agreed upon restaurant. How can we have scheduling conflicts? We're on vacation!

Telephone calls to brother Matthew's condo go unanswered meaning he is either in the shower or ran to Wal-Mart. Brother John's two boys were hungry as soon as they got off the beach so John took them to McDonalds. Thus, there is some concern the two boys may not be in the mood to sit for any length of time at a restaurant table watching other people eat. Sister Jo-Ann wants to go but she must wait for her friend from Connecticut to arrive. Brother Josh's dilemma is that daughter Katie just wants ice cream. Son Kevin just has to have pizza. And then for the real wrench in the works.

Once we've finally determined *who's* going and *when*, we have to deal with the fact that half of our family is vegan! It is not easy to find a restaurant that caters to tastes ranging from lobster tails to tofu.

We go through this frustrating ritual for each and every excursion be it eating, sightseeing, shopping, a trip to the casino or a simple family get-together at one of our cottages. Why we go through this baffles me. It's not as though we didn't know we were coming here this year! We've had 351 days to make these plans. We know every restaurant and what they serve. All year long we talk about going to the casinos, Watch Hill, Mystic Seaport, the harbor tour aboard the Southland and having relaxing cocktails on the outside deck of the Ocean House. Yet, when we actually get to Weekapaug we act like confused tourists who are there for the first time.

It is ironic then, that we have *never* planned what is arguably the one activity each of us looks most forward to -- a walk on the beach. We don't wake up in the morning and say, "As soon as I get to the beach today, I'm taking a nice, long walk." No -- one's desire to go for a walk on the beach is usually triggered by what is happening around you once you're on the beach and the state of mind you are in at the moment. You may be sitting in a beach chair, book in hand and you find yourself nodding off. You decide a walk on the beach will snap you out of your lethargy. Working too intensely on your tan can also be a catalyst for a beach walk. You can lay out for only so long before the sun's rays make you so uncomfortably hot that only a walk amidst the cool ocean breeze will bring relief. Sometimes you walk because you have been abandoned. Some of your family are in the water, some went back to the cottage for lunch while others went for a walk, leaving you all alone.

So, off you go on the same walk you've taken hundreds of times, past the same oceanfront cottages. You have no idea how long or how far you will walk but always in the back of your mind you know that however long you've walked when you decided to turn around is how long it's going to take you to make it back to your blanket.

The first minute of your walk is not really an official part of the walk. Your first few steps are dedicated to maneuvering around other people's blankets as you make your way to the ocean's edge. Once you've distanced yourself from the people on your own beach you must walk past the six or seven groups of people who have spread their blankets further down the beach away from the main crowd. It is these people who will be talking about you as you pass. How do you know? Because you do the same thing when a beachwalker walks past you and your group! Who do we make fun of? The forty-ish bleach blonde trying to stuff 30 excess pounds into a bikini she has no business wearing is always fair game. Also good for a laugh is Penelope Pacer. She's the 20-something who walks as fast as most of us can run, checking her watch every 15 seconds to see if she's making good time. Then there is the buxom teenager in the thong. When she walks past, every man who is sitting on the beach beside his wife says to himself, "Boy am I glad I'm wearing these sunglasses. My wife thinks I'm asleep!" Then there is the 65-year old all-too-tanned and all-too-hairy European -looking gentlemen with all-too-much Bryl Cream in his hair and sporting a Speedo bathing suit. We are merciless with our snide remarks about his "bunch of grapes." So now that you're on your walk, you too are fair game -- but you don't care. Once away from the crowd and the gawkers and the talkers the shoreline is yours. Now it's just you and your thoughts. The walk is like your own personal confessional with no priest to pass judgement on your deeds. You can think any thought. You can be honest with yourself. You can relive past personal victories as well as defeats. You can plan your future. You vow that your walk here next year will find you in much different circumstances than this year. Along the way you feel the urge to wade knee deep into the ocean and marvel at the vastness of the sea and sky. You pick up things -- rocks, shells -- and then drop them back to the sand. You see someone walking toward you and as you pass each other you wonder what set of life circumstances brought that person here. Are they getting over a divorce? Are they contemplating a career move? Or are they simply taking some time alone to reflect on family, health and how happy they are to be at this spot? They wonder the same about you. What a wonderful experience it would be if we had the nerve to walk up to that person and say, “Hi, what are you thinking about right now?” I am sure a nice conversation and a new friendship would result. But we don’t. We’re too afraid, perhaps of rejection. We’re two ships who pass in the light.

You eventually decide to turn around and head back to your beach. Up ahead you see a person walking toward you -- the same person who was walking toward you earlier, only now you are both going the other way. They too, turned around. As you pass you nod to each other, each realizing you were impolite for not saying hello or smiling the first time you passed each other.

As you get closer to your blanket you pass the gawkers and talkers, most of whom are now face down on their towels and have no idea you are making your return trip. However, a few of them are still staring and when you make quick eye contact with them they smile sheepishly and wave as if to say, “Yeah, you caught us. We’re still checking you out.”

You make it back to your blanket and gaze out to the ocean and wonder where the family is planning to go out to dinner tonight.

The Ring

It is a rare man who, during the course of a marriage has not heard his wife say, "Jeez, sometimes I think you're worse than the kids!" I heard it more than once and in each case, for as much as I hate to admit it, the accusation was justified. I heard it most frequently when I just couldn't wait 10 more minutes for dinner to be ready and just *had* to rummage through the refrigerator for a slice of cheese, a pickle or a bite of last night's leftover chicken. Playing the stereo at full volume would also guarantee an annoyed spousal outburst. We men can't understand why our wives frown upon deafening decibles of Hendrix, The Who, Foghat and Lynyrd Skynyrd as we prance around the house playing power chords on our air guitars. Yes, we're guilty and we promise to try to control ourselves next time.

However, there is one childish act we are famous for and for which we should not be held accountable. We cannot help going into a frenzied panic when we hear the ring -- the ring as in the ring of the ice cream man as his truck slowly makes its way down the street in front of the cottage. It doesn't matter if we are watching television, helping with dinner or are engaged in a deep, serious conversation with our wives -- the ring freezes us in our tracks and then causes us to blurt out, "Where's my wallet!? Get my wallet! Hurry!"

When I do this, the urgency in my voice sets off a stampede by my nieces and nephews who race for the front door screaming, "I want a Push-Up!", "Oohh, I want a Nutty Buddy!", and "I'm gettin' a Rocket popsicle!" But as the children push and shove their way through the front door and out onto the porch they let out a collective, "Awww! We missed him!" At first glance, the kids appear to be right in their assessment -- the truck is far down the street and the sound of the bell begins to fade. It is now time for me to save the situation and light up the long faces with a bit of ice cream truck wisdom gleaned from years of experience. I explain to them that the reason the ice cream man drives down the street slowly without stopping is to get your attention. He *wants* you to hear the bells. He *wants* you to know he's on your street. He knows that by the time he drives to the end of the road and turns around, you will have had enough time to get your money and congregate curbside.

My experience in the television news business gives me special insight into the psychology the ice cream man is using. We, in television use a technique known as the 'tease.' This is when we show you a compelling piece of video such as an explosives expert lighting dynamite to blow up an old bridge. During the tease we never show you the actual explosion -- rather, the anchorman excitedly intones, "When we come back we'll show you how to make a bridge disappear in three seconds! You won't want to miss it! Stay with us!" After a great tease like that we *know* you'll be back because you just *gotta* see it!

The ice cream man is teasing you. He is almost taunting you as he rings his bell and drives past your cottage. In television news tease terms, he is essentially saying, "Hurry up and get your money and get out to the street because in five minutes I'll be pulling up in front of your place and you won't want to miss me!" Then, as though it were scripted, the minute you and your clan congregate curbside the ice cream truck comes into view way down the street -- right on cue. But your excitement quickly turns to disappointment when you see 10 other families streetside and the ice cream man has to take care of all of them before he gets to you! These are the very families you spent the day with on the beach. You and the other adults chatted, shared newspapers and even took beach walks together. Your children played with their children in the sand and surf. But right now you hate them all.

When the ice cream truck finally gets to your cottage you realize the vehicle is nothing more than a converted milk delivery truck with a big picture window cut into the side of it. The driver is a high school kid wearing cutoff jeans and a t-shirt. He puts the truck in park, walks behind the driver's seat and back to the window and bends down and stares at you, never so much as asking what you would like. It is up to *you* to initiate the communication by telling him your order because he has no desire to exchange pleasantries with you.

It is this sight that makes me long for the 'real' ice cream man of my childhood in the early 60's -- the Good Humor Man. Good Humor was, and still is an official ice cream company. But back then the company had a fleet of impressive Good Humor trucks which were essentially freezers on wheels. Each truck had the Good Humor logo emblazoned on the side. The driver was required to wear the official Good Humor uniform -- white pants, white short-sleeved-shirt, shiny black shoes and a real change dispenser hanging from his belt. On the side of the truck was the official Good Humor ice cream menu complete with pictures and prices. When the driver pulled up to your house he would get out and walk to the back of the vehicle where he took your order. He then opened a small freezer door at the back of the truck and without ever looking inside he reached in and through all the smoke and condensation pouring out of the freezer he always pulled out your exact order.

I quickly snap back to present-day reality. The kids are still busy ordering their Push-Ups, Nutty Buddys and Rocket popsicles. I scan the side of the truck where there are pictures of the various treats and I decide I'd like the 'Jaws' popsicle -- the one shaped like a shark. Of course, that one has a big Magic Marker 'X' through it and next to it is the word "OUT."

I decide to settle for an old favorite and tell the ice cream man, "I'll have a Toasted Almond." He looks at me inquisitively with an expression that says, "Dude -- a Toasted *what*?" I settle for a Nutty Buddy and head back to the cottage to reminisce about the good old days of the Good Humor Man. Maybe I'll feel better if I listen to some Hendrix on my 8-Track player.

Clamming

I've discovered that one of the best ways to cope with a mid-January Wisconsin blizzard is to bring out the photo album filled with the nearly 300 pictures I took in Weekapaug the previous August. My son Michael and I, along with his two friends who joined us on the vacation savor every shot and relive each moment frozen in 35 millimeter time. For the next half hour we're all in Weekapaug again.

Looking at the photos puts me in full beach mood to the point that I must grab a pen and pad and furiously make a list of all the things I want to make sure I do when I get there next year. Movie night with my young nieces and nephews is a must. We first run out either for hot fudge sundaes or pizza -- kids' choice -- and bring it back to the cottage where we drape ourselves over the couch or melt into the easy chairs to enjoy the evening's VHS selection -- Uncle Tom's choice. This year it was *Monster Squad*.

The sightseeing boat tour of Narragansett harbor aboard the Southland also makes the list. Although I've taken the tour countless times I can never get enough of chugging along the harbor coastline past fishing villages, fishing trawlers, fishermen unloading their catch destined for the processing plant, beautiful seaside cottages, beaches, restaurants, lighthouses and even the shark cage that sits on one of the docks.

A night of board games or card-playing ranks high on the list also. Brother Matthew makes smoothies in the blender with Bacardi's One-Fifty-One. There is much laughter and I get a kick out of watching my brothers choke on their once- a-year cigars.

In recent years the annual Charlestown Seafood Festival has been added to the lineup. My list continues with kayaking on the ocean, drinks on the deck of the Ocean House in Watch Hill and shining brother John's powerful searchlight into the Weekapaug Breachway at night to watch the lobsters, crabs, eels, starfish, jellyfish and even seahorses put on their nocturnal performances.

There is one other item that makes the list every year but I never seem to get around to doing it. Clamming.

Ironically, of all the activities on my list clamming requires the least amount of planning, equipment or effort. The only real requirement for a clamming excursion is a Shellfish License. Vacationers can purchase a two-week license for somewhere around $11 from city hall, bait shops or select stores.

Once you are licensed and legal your clamming excursion can be as simple or as involved as you want to make it. During my childhood years in Weekapaug clamming was a big production -- a family affair that included Mom, Dad, my five brothers and sisters plus any relatives or visiting friends who wished to join us. The first order of business was to fill the large Scotch cooler with ice, soda and sandwiches. The boys were put in charge of carrying the clam rakes -- four long-handled and two short, handheld ones. We also brought with us a bushel basket buoyed by an innertube. As we raked for clams the floating basket was tethered by a ten-foot rope to a belt loop on our cutoff jean shorts. This saved us the trouble of having to wade 100 yards to shore to drop each fresh-caught clam in the basket. Attached to the basket by a six-inch piece of string was the clam ring which was given to you when you purchased the clamming licenses. If a clam fit through the ring the clam was too small and had to be returned to the sea. Heaven help the clammer who was caught by a Department of Environmental Management warden without a license or with a clam in his basket that fit through the ring.

For two to three hours we would stand in thigh-to-waist-deep water carefully making well-defined patterns with our rakes across the soft mud much like a gardener raking through a plot of soft dirt that was soon to be planted. With each stroke came the hope of feeling and hearing the 'scrape.' The scrape meant there was the distinct possibility that you had hit a clam. Each rake had five teeth that were about five inches long which allowed the clammer to dig behind the object he hit and pull it up along with five pounds of mud. Then, three or four dips of the rake into the water would ultimately wash away all the mud and expose whatever object it was that you dug up. Sometimes the object would bring momentary excitement followed by disappointment when it turned out to be the empty shell of a clam that had long ago made its final migration with the tide. Sometimes there would be shock and fear at the end of your rake when the object turned out to be a horseshoe crab that had buried itself into the mud. The creature's shell looks like a helmet, its underside is a mass of moving legs and its eight-inch long spiked tail is flailing up and down in search of a soft spot on your body to penetrate.

Other possibilities at the end of your rake include a large oyster shell. Or the ultimate insult -- a rock -- which has all the properties of a clam -- the scraping sounds, the feel and the look. But when all the mud is cleaned off of it your happiness turns to heartbreak. These disappointments are all forgotten, however, when a beautiful, sparkling, light gray clam emerges from the mud ball. No one in our family has ever caught a clam and not waved it in the air shouting, "Hey!" This is not a wise move, however, because immediately, the rest of the clammers who have had no luck begin making their way toward your spot.

Sometimes we would see other families clamming nearby, but they had no rakes. Rather, they had small boards. These people were schooled in the art of 'fanning' for clams. They would kneel in the water and fan the board back and forth over the mud. They would then wait a few seconds for the water to clear up and if they were lucky a clam or two would be sitting exposed atop the mud. I was never a fan of fanning.

In my adult years I have discovered a way to catch clams that is not as hard on your back as raking is. We fan with our flipflops. As my brothers and I stand in knee-deep water in the salt pond chatting we fan the mud from left to right with one of our flipflops. After 30 seconds of fanning we let the water clear and there they are -- clams laying at our feet!

For me it is the thrill of the hunt that is most important. I pick up each clam, study it, marvel at its coloration, enjoy its coolness in my hand and then I return the clam to where it belongs -- the soft, sandy bottom of the ocean. Am I a vegetarian? No. Do I eat clams? Yes. I truly enjoy eating clam strips, clam fritters, fried clams and clam cakes. I have no problem eating these clam dishes because I have no personal connection to the clams contained in them. But the clams I catch myself are different. They give me great joy -- a feeling of being in touch with the ocean and its creatures. These clams I cannot eat. These clams made their journey from the ocean, fought their way up the breachway and made it to the calm of the salt pond. How cruel it would be to reward the joy they brought to me by introducing them to a bottle of cocktail sauce.

Night Waves

Beach cottages are notorious for being nighttime hotboxes where sleep is almost impossible. No matter how tired we are after a long day of sun, surf, walks on the beach, good food and ample doses of alcohol we always dread bedtime. Not just because bedtime marks the passing of another day in Weekapaug, but because we know that a hellish night is in store.

There is no such thing as an air conditioner in a cottage so at bedtime ventilation is accomplished only by opening the lone bedroom window which does nothing except to allow the 80-degree, muggy, sticky, stifling, salt-laden night air into the room. You toss. You turn. You throw blankets and sheets to the floor. You shed as much clothing as you dare. Nothing works. All you can do is await the merciful arrival of morning.

There is, however, one good thing that comes of this nautical, nocturnal nightmare. The open window allows in the sound of the ocean waves at night. Waves at night, experienced from your bed have a sound and feel so much different than the waves you saw and played in earlier in the day. Day waves are a sight to behold and provide an experience to be enjoyed. Your beach chair serves as a front row seat to nature's perfect performance. You can see a swell building 500 yards out at sea. As it gets closer it becomes larger until it becomes a moving mountain bearing down on the beach. When the swell reaches shallow water the base remains wide and strong while the top grows taller, narrows and forms a whitecapped peak. The bright sunshine allows you to see right through the face of the wave. Then, as though too impatient to get to shore, the peak speeds ahead of the base and crashes in an explosion of foam that rushes relentlessly toward the beach. It is much like watching your favorite film for the twentieth time. You know how it ends, yet you watch it with the same anticipation and excitement you had the first time you saw it. It is a matinee like no other and the encores continue for as long as you'll stay to watch them.

The midnight show however, is much different. For one thing, the curtain remains closed for the entire performance. You can hear but you cannot see. Your seat has been changed. Instead of a beach chair in the front row your vantage point is now just a bed and an open window. As you lie in the darkness you hear an ominous rumbling followed by a huge crash. It is as if two huge dinosaurs are doing battle on the beach. Your mind cannot fathom what sort of mayhem is occurring in the waters you frolicked in just hours earlier. You try to imagine what it must look like. Dark, choppy water. Menacing whitecaps. Waves larger than you've ever seen slamming and banging into each other. It is an enraged, violent sea.

Yes, the sea is angry and perhaps rightfully so. If it could talk to us here is what I think it would say.

"Do not fear my temper tantrum. It is for your good that I do it. If I crash violently to shore it is only to toss back at you that which you defiled me with this day. It is my way of angrily lashing out at you who violated me for no other reason than your carelessness. I am throwing back to shore your styrofoam cups, your plastic bags, your juice boxes, your candy wrappers, your plastic bottles and your cruel fishing lines. Once I have given you back what is yours I will take back what is mine. After I crash to shore and recede I will take back the large, dead striper you walked

past on your beach walk. Did its demise come as the result of a fisherman's hook? I will take back the dead crabs. They didn't survive the ordeal of your child's pail where there was no food and only a small amount of water in which the oxygen dissipated quickly in the hot sun. I will take back the jellyfish that met with the same fate. I will take back the dead seagull that I know did not die of natural causes. Was it a stick, a football or a Frisbee that broke its neck? I return to you what is yours. I take back what is mine. Tomorrow when you come to the beach it will be fresh, clean, rejuvenated and pristine. So sleep peacefully and when you arrive tomorrow I will be what you expect me to be -- calm, shining, peaceful and beautiful. Please give some thought to the way you treat me and mine."

We finally fall asleep.

Digging in deeper and deeper 'til they disappear

Feet In The Mud

There are certain experiences I enjoy as an adult as much as I did when I was a child. One such experience is when I stand at the ocean's edge and watch my feet slowly sink into the mud.

Children make a game of it. They stand in ankle-deep water and watch as the foaming surf from a breaking wave rushes over the tops of their feet and then recedes, taking with it some of the sandy mud from beneath the children's feet. After only a few minutes the child is buried past his ankles in mud at which point he's had enough of the game and runs off in pursuit of some other beach activity.

Mothers take a more relaxed and intelligent approach to this endeavor. They position a comfortable beach chair in the ankle-deep water and enjoy some summer reading while the sand and surf swallow their feet.

For men, this is a group activity that just sort of happens. Last year it began when my brother Josh and I stood in knee-deep water keeping an eye on his daughter and son, Katie and Kevin who were playing in the waves. To our right were longtime friends Peter and Jeff who were watching *their* kids as well. Although we see Peter and Jeff for only two weeks out of the entire year, their families and ours have been meeting in Weekapaug for so many years that it feels like we see each other regularly the rest of the year. When we spot each other for the first time, knowing smiles and sincere handshakes are exchanged. Almost in unison we exclaim, “Well, here we are!” Peter’s thick New England accent comes out as “Well, here we ahhhh!” We understand him nonetheless. The four of us form a semi-circle facing the ocean so that we can watch the kids and still somewhat face each other to converse at the same time. The next 20 minutes are spent catching up on each other’s lives and discussing what has changed in Weekapaug since last year -- a new cottage went up on Breach Drive, Vincent sold the Breachway Market but he stopped in the other day and there’s talk of replacing the Weekapaug Bridge. We talk. Time goes by. The waves wash over our feet. Before we know it we’re all six inches shorter than when we began talking.

When there is a lull in the conversation we look out to sea. The kids are okay, the fog has lifted allowing us to see clearly all the way to Block Island and a huge barge is making its way across the horizon. We all comment, wondering where it is from and what its cargo might be. We also can’t resist asking each other if there have been any shark sightings. As we stand in place we dig our feet in deeper much like a baseball player does at homeplate as he gets ready to bat.

Inevitably, this mutual admiration huddle is broken. The usual cause is a child who is tired of the ocean and wants a sandwich or a spouse who needs you to go back to the cottage to get the cooler. So, with a mighty, yet reluctant pull, we extract first one foot and then the other from their muddy graves. We try to admire our handywork (or footywork) by looking back at the spot upon which we just stood. Unfortunately, the very second we removed our feet from the mud, the sand and surf combined to fill the holes and smoothed them over leaving no evidence that we were ever there. In any case we adjourn to our respective beach blankets where we sit within mere yards of each other. Jeff reads the newspaper. Peter buries his face in a book or magazine. Josh reaches for his camcorder to make sure every second of Katie and Kevin's time at the beach is documented for posterity. I decide to take a walk to the breachway.

Thus, our annual Return-To-Weekapaug ritual is complete and for the moment, forgotten. I wonder where the other three guys will be when our wonderful metatarsals-in-the-mud moment crosses their minds again? It happened for me in early December during a boring meeting when my foot fell asleep. I and it longed to be somewhere else.

Shower

My home has all the modern conveniences and comforts found in many homes. It has central air conditioning, a fireplace, two-and-a-half bathrooms, a recreation room, a computer, a big screen TV and we allowed ourselves to spend a little extra for the bathtub that had the water jets. But I kick myself every time I think of the fact that I didn't have my homebuilder install the one thing that would have made me happy above all else. I want an outside shower! Even if I never used it, I would always be reminded of the other place near and dear to my heart that has an outside shower -- my cottage in Weekapaug.

Almost every seashore vacation cottage has one. However, the owners installed it not as a convenience or comfort but rather as a practical nautical necessity. Invariably, one of the items on the list of Cottage Rules that are posted on the refrigerator door is a request that reads something like, "Please use the outside shower to rinse off sand before using the indoor shower". This request is designed to make sure we don't drag sand all through the cottage and to prevent sand from clogging up the indoor pipes and drains.

Some outside showers are enclosed and look like an outhouse that is connected to the cottage. Others are exposed, simply consisting of a showerhead, two faucets and a soap dish sticking out of the side of the cottage. Common to both types are the things you find on the cement slab floor and in the soap dish. On the floor you will often find a rolled up t-shirt or bathing suit belonging to one of the children of the previous renters. It is covered with sand and dead mosquitoes and a beetle or two. The other personal item most commonly found is a bathing cap which tells you that someone over the age of 75 has been here recently.

In the soap dish is a half-used-up white bar of soap, usually Ivory, sitting in watery, gooey Ivory soap syrup. The underside of this soap bar is mushy and slimy. Balanced on the soap dish next to the bar of soap is a plastic bottle of White Rain shampoo. It is two-thirds empty and seems to have a consistency closer to water than soap. You pick up the bar of soap and begin to rinse it off when a disgusting thought hits you and you say to yourself, "Why are you touching the soap? You have *no* idea where that soap has been!" Then comes the doubly-disgusting thought as you answer your own question -- "Yuk! I *do* know where that soap has been!" I suppose I am partial to outside showers that are enclosed because they afford you the ability to take off your bathing suit so that you can rinse off *all* the sand. An unenclosed shower forces you to stick the bar of soap down your bathing suit in search of any hidden sand. I also prefer enclosed showers because they provide the opportunity for a few minutes of mental mischief. Through the crack in the latched door you can see people walking on the street in front of the cottage or the next door neighbors grilling burgers. I peek out through the crack and in soapy silence I think to myself, "I wonder what those people would do if they knew they were being spied on by somebody who's just 25 feet away and naked?"

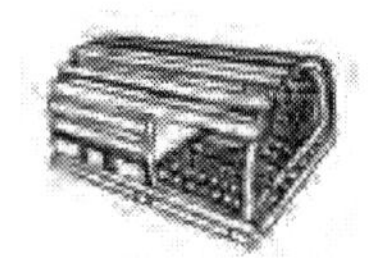

Minnows!

I have rented at least 10 different cottages in Weekapaug over the years and check-in day has found each one to be neat and clean. I attribute this to a couple of things. First, we renters live by an unwritten beach code that demands we leave the place cleaner than we found it. Thus, it stands to reason that the last renter of the summer gets a really clean cottage! We also clean because of fear of not being allowed to rent the place next year. Another reason cottages are so clean is that after we've scoured, swept and straightened, a cleaning service comes in just before the next renters arrive. Cottage owners hire cleaning services out of fear that we won't return next year to again pay the $1300 weekly rental rate.

But for all the cleaning that goes on they are still *cottages* and not year 'round homes. No one does spring cleaning. No one does fall cleaning. By late August or early September the cottages are boarded up and sit empty until mid- May or early June.

In the summer of 2002 my brother Matthew arrived from Delaware and spent the first week of his vacation at his beachfront timeshare townhouse. He noticed that on Breach Drive which is the street where most of the family rents, there was a small cottage that stood empty. Matt thought this would be the perfect place to rent for his second week stay. The cottage owner, who has several properties on Breach Drive happened by. After a five-minute chat he and Matt went inside where Matt wrote a check at the kitchen table for $600 and the deal was done. Although the cottage was clean it was well known in our vacation rental circle that this particular landlord would never spend a dime on the Merry Maids.

One evening later that week we sent out for pizza and decided that Matt's cottage would be the place we'd all congregate. It was the kind of night that the beach is all about -- 20 of us crammed into Matt's kitchen and adjoining living room. There was soda, beer, wine and eight cardboard pizza boxes. Two pizza boxes lay open on the kitchen countertop next to the sink, three more on the kitchen table and the other three on the couch.

We adults knew that before we could get into serious pizza and beer mode the kids would have to be taken care of first. So the four children -- Jonathan, Justin, Katie and Kevin -- took their places of honor at the kitchen table. One of the adults reached up into the kitchen cabinets to get plates for the children.

Kevin sat patiently as his father, Josh, peeled a piece of pizza from the bottom of one of the cardboard boxes when suddenly Kevin excitedly shouted, "Hey, there's minnows on my plate!" We all looked and sure enough, we saw what appeared to be several minnows darting across Kevin's plate as though they were swimming in a tide pool. But Kevin's plate obviously had no water in it. Then came another shout, this one from an adult -- "Oh, God! Silverfish!" My American Heritage Dictionary defines a silverfish as a silvery, wingless insect that often causes extensive damage to bookbindings and starched clothing. My dictionary, complete with an accompanying picture of said creature, failed to mention that silverfish also cause extensive damage to appetites.

A check of the cabinets found silverfish crawling all over everything -- on dishes and inside bowls, coffee cups and drinking glasses. The adults who had already downed half a beer from one of the cottage drinking glasses quickly set the glass down and wondered what else beside beer had made it down their throat.

Paper cups and styrofoam plates got us through the rest of the evening.

AUGUST2003

HIGH TIDE TABLE
for

WATCH HILL, AI

DAY IGHT SAVING TIME: (Starts 416 2AM

ADD 6HOURS FOR OW TIDE

Date	AM	PM	Date	AM	PM
1	11:32	11:47	17	12:37	12;57
2		12:21	18	1;19	1;39
3	12:37	1:12	19	2:01	2:22
4	1130	2:05	20	2:47	3.'08
5	2:25	3:02	21	3:38	4:01
6	3:24	4:03	22	4:37	5:03
7	4:27	5:09	23	5:39	6:03
8	5:34	6:14	24	8I38	6:56
9	<>38	7;13	25	7 -	7;41
10	7:36	8:07	26	8:09	8:24
11	8:28	856	27	8 2	9:08
12	9:16	9:42	28	9:35	9:52
13	11k02	10:27	29	10:20	10!38
14	10:47	11:11	30	11:07	11:26
15	1131	1154	31	11:57	
16		12:15			

FROM WATCH HIL, AITO:

Westerly, Pawcatuck River	-21 min.
Noank,Mystic River	-51 m
Stonington	-40 min.
Old saybrook Point	-1hr. 5 min.

High Tide Table
for
Watch **Hill, RI**

Complimets of

WEEKAPAUG
BAIT & TACKLE
SHOP

Weekapaug, Rhode Island

E-mail:

servIce@weekapaugbaJtandtackla.com

(401) 322-

A Wave From Nowhere

If the weather forecast is the thing we pay attention to most while in Weekapaug, the tides are a close second. Each day, concern about the status of the tide is so ingrained into our collective beach psyche that we've even created our own 'tide' language to discuss it. You will never hear one of us ask, "Is it high tide or low tide?" We simply say, "What's it doin'?" and everyone knows what we mean. "What's it doin'?" will have everything to do with how we plan our day.

Those of us who are seasoned tide watchers need only look at the waterline on the rocks at the breachway to determine whether the tide is coming in or going out. We can also pinpoint with some degree of accuracy the time the tide will either be all the way in or out. My three brothers -- John, Matt and Josh -- can even recognize a slack tide. Slack tide is the lull that lasts just a few minutes between tides when the tide is neither coming in nor going out. It is as if the tide flow is taking a short rest before it has to turn around and go back the other way

For those not so adept at being able to eyeball the status of a tide, every cottage has a tide chart that somebody picked up at the local bait shop. This chart, mainly used by fishermen and boaters, tells you the exact minute of each day's high and low tides for the entire summer season of May through September.

Once we've consulted with John, Matt, Josh or the chart, we make our plans that quite literally go with the tide. Each tide is your friend or your enemy depending upon the activities you'd like to partake in. Here, for example, is what an 8:03 A.M. low tide means to everyone involved. The beachlovers know that the morning surf will be all too calm with no waves since high tide won't be in until around two in the afternoon. This would be a good morning to get the grocery shopping done or to run up to one of the Watch Hill shops for sunglasses and beach reading. Noon or one o'clock would be the perfect time to arrive at the beach to take advantage of the tide and waves building to their two o'clock peak.

For clammers, the 8:03 A.M. low tide is a call to action. Clamming is best done at complete low tide as the shallow waters allow for maximum access to the muddy clambeds that are teeming with quahogs and steamers.

Kayakers know that any attempt to head out into the ocean via the breachway between 8 A.M. and 2 P.M. will be a battle. They will literally be paddling against the incoming tide. Smart kayakers like my three brothers, slip through the breachway and out into the ocean at slack tide right around 8 A.M. Then after a morning of kayaking on the ocean their return trip is a breeze as they ride the incoming tide back home.

For children, high tide brings multiple pleasures. First, the waves are huge. Body surfing is at its best. Riding a wave on an inflatable raft is both exhilarating and frightening as the mountain of water envelopes, jettisons, tosses and sometimes tumbles the craft. High tide also brings in thousands of crabs into the breachway and its inlets. With a simple drop line and a fishhead a child's bucket is full of crabs in no time.

Yet, for as important a role tides play in our daily beach lives there are some people who are oblivious to Mother Nature's every-six-hour cycle that has not missed a beat in thousands of years. While I am sure these people understand that what goes up must come down, they haven't grasped the concept of what goes out must come in. These are the people who arrive at the beach when the tide is all the way out and they set up their beach blanket, towels, umbrella, chairs and cooler just a few yards from the water's edge. Once they are settled in they take on a self- satisfied, almost smug demeanor thinking they've got the best seat in the house. They can't help but turn around to make sure those of us who are set up further away from the water acknowledge that they got the front row. In their smugness however, these people never thought to ask themselves, "If all those people got here before we did, why are they sitting so far back?" The incoming tide will soon provide their answer.

As these people sun themselves, read their books and newspapers, frolic in the waves and go for long walks, they don't seem to notice that the ocean is slowly and steadily creeping toward their blanket. Then suddenly, when they are not expecting it, a huge wave comes out of nowhere, roars up the sandy beach and floods the blanket, towels, the books, newspapers and chairs. They all jump up in shock and begin pulling all their belongings back away from the water as if in full retreat.

For the moment, we seasoned beach sitters revel in their misfortune to the point that we almost want to shout, "There! That'll teach ya!" But our revelry soon turns to misery and annoyance when we realize these beach novices have retreated

The View From The Blanket into our laps. What minutes ago was a wide open, sandy plot in front of our blanket is now occupied by wet towels, a muddy, sandy blanket, hastily folded chairs, beach toys and complete strangers who half expect us to back up to accommodate them.

We steadfastly hold our ground, refusing to budge and we pretend not to notice them. We suppress the urge to say, "This is musical chairs, beach style. And you lost!"

Long ago, the man in the middle made his way up this steep dune in the author's arms

Time Passages

To get to the private beach reserved for cottages on the street that my family rents on, one must pass through the gate of a chain link fence and then walk up a relatively steep, sandy dune about 100 yards long.

The walk is no picnic as the sand is thick and deep and makes each step a chore. Many of us have had to go back a step or two to recover a lost flipflop. The journey becomes even more difficult if one is carrying a beach chair, cooler, umbrella, children's beach toys, or, for that matter, a child.

One afternoon as I made the trek carrying just a towel and a book I found my progress being impeded by a family of four who I quickly caught up with and whose destination was the same as mine. A little girl, probably five years old led the way, running ahead of her mother who was carrying a beach chair and an overloaded beach bag. Behind Mom was Dad, holding a three-year- old boy in his arm and trying to make the climb through the hot sand of the steeply sloping dune, struggling much like someone on skis trying to walk up an icy slope.

The father sensed I was on his heels, turned to me and said something like, "Oh sorry, we're kind of slowing up the parade." He started to move to the side of the narrow path to let me pass.

Fifty yards ahead of us at the peak of the dune was a group of young men whose ages ranged from 18 to 21. They were all about 6'2" or 6'3" and each weighed well over 200 pounds. They all had a two-day growth of beard and carried towels, coolers, boom boxes and CD players. It was the proverbial group you 'wouldn't want to mess with.'

As the father offered to let me pass, I said to him, "No, no, take your time." And then I said, "See those guys at the top of the hill? See the one in the black t-shirt? That's my son and 18 years ago I carried him up this same path just like you're doing". At that point the Dad realized that this walk up the dune was going to last a lifetime. I looked up proudly at my son standing atop the dune looking like the king of the beach. I suppose it's every father's dream to see their children make it to the top on their own.

Your Weekapaug

I don't like thinking about the fact that my Weekapaug days are numbered. With only a few breaks in the string, most of my 51 years have been hyphenated by a two-week stay there. The odds do not favor my enjoying another 51.

Having come to terms with this fact I now find myself clinging for dear life to each new visit and letting go gets harder and harder with each passing year. I think about Weekapaug more than I used to. I relive and savor the memories more than I used to. I am less patient as I wait for winter's winds to blow the calendar's pages to August. Each Weekapaug visit now holds more meaning. I try to suck every ounce of juice out of those 14 precious days. I take more pictures.

My wish for you is that this, the end of my Weekapaug is the beginning of yours. Throughout the time I was writing this book, friends, coworkers and acquaintances got wind of the fact that I was 'doing a book.' When they would ask me what it was going to be about, my answer invariably triggered the same response many times over -- "You're writing *my* book!" And they were right. I *was* writing their book because everyone has the desire to write about their cherished vacation memories. But while desire is one thing, actually doing it is quite another.

Since those who know me know that I work on television and that I am not an author, their next question was, "How did you do it?" *The View From The Blanket* was born August 1, 2000 in the kitchen of my cottage on the Winnapaug Salt Pond during a torrential rainstorm (see Rainy Days). The birth was the result of a union between a pen and a can of Budweiser. As I cursed the clouds I began to write down my thoughts about the downpour -- thoughts that I knew were going through the minds of every

Mom and Dad at every cottage at that very minute. As I wrote, all kinds of beach thoughts flooded my brain and suddenly I couldn't write fast enough to keep up with all of them -- walking on the beach, clamming, the Breachway Market, crabbing, waves at night, sharks and scores of other experiences and memories. Before I knew it I had filled the page and with each passing day more thoughts and ideas were added.

It wasn't until I returned to my home in Green Bay that I first dared think the thought -- "Hey, I think there's a book here." I was not convinced of it until I started telling my brothers and sisters about the things I had written down. Each chimed in excitedly with, "Oh, you gotta write about....," "...remember to do a chapter on....," and "..don't forget the time...." As I floated my idea past friends and fellow vactioners their responses were, "How soon is it comin' out?" and "Where can I buy a copy?" I had enough sense to realize that their excitement and enthusiasm had little to do with *my* book. It had everything to do with *their* book. My book was their book -- the book they and all of us have in our minds and hearts that is waiting to be written.

While I hope you have enjoyed my ravings, rantings and 'reminiscings', my greatest reward would be the hope that my Weekapaug moved you to write your Weekapaug. I am not suggesting you write a book, although you certainly could! You might start as I did -- jotting down memories to be later turned into essays in your own words. Ask other family members to do the same. Soon, you will have a collection of beautiful, personal essays, each representing the innermost thoughts, reflections and memories of each individual contributor. It is this collection of essays that should be the first thing you pack for the next trip to the cottage. Then on a chilly summer night as you all sink into the worn out sofas and chairs of the musty, yet so comfortable cottage living room, pour the cocktails and then pour out your hearts as you read your reminiscings to each other. You will see the vacation spot you thought you knew everything about through different eyes and hearts. I hope it moves you to tears. I hope it puts you in a state of gratitude, appreciation and reflection. I hope it puts you in a state of realizing how lucky you are to have experienced and shared all these wonderful memories over the years with the ones you love.

I hope it puts you in a state of Weekapaug.